Cycle Rides

Peak District
& the Heart of England

D0474903

Publisher: David Watchus
Managing Editor: Isla Love
Senior Editor: Donna Wood
Senior Designer: Kat Mead
Picture Research: Lesley Grayson
Cartographic Editor: Geoff Chapman
Cartographic Production: Anna Thompson

Produced by AA Publishing
© Automobile Association Developments l

Published by AA Publishing (a trading name of Automobile Association Developments Limited, whose registered office is Fanum House, Basing View, Basingstoke, Hampshire RG21 4EA; registered number 1878835).

 This product includes mapping data licensed from the Ordnance Survey® with the permission of the Controller of Her Majesty's Stationery Office. © Crown copyright 2007. All rights reserved. Licence number 100021153.

A03033c

ISBN-10: 0-7495-5193-3
ISBN-13: 978-0-7495-5193-3

A CIP catalogue record for this book is available from the British Library.

The contents of this book are believed correct at the time of printing. Nevertheless, the publishers cannot be held responsible for any errors or omissions or for changes in the details given in this book or for the consequences of any reliance on the information it provides. We have tried to ensure accuracy in this book, but things do change and we would be grateful if readers could advise us of any inaccuracies they may encounter. This does not affect your statutory rights.

We have taken all reasonable steps to ensure that the cycle rides in this book are safe and achievable by people with a reasonable level of fitness. However, all outdoor activities involve a degree of risk and the publishers accept no responsibility for any injuries caused to readers whilst following these cycle rides. For advice on cycling in safety, see pages 10–11.
Some of the cycle rides may appear in other AA books and publications.

Visit AA Publishing's website www.theAA.com/travel

Colour reproduction by Keene Group, Andover
Printed in Italy by G Canale & C SPA

Cycle Rides

Peak District
& the Heart of England

Contents

Locator map   5

Introduction to the Peak District & the Heart of England   6

Using this book   8

About the pubs   9

Cycling in safety   10

1   The jaws of Longdendale, Derbyshire   12

2   The Upper Derwent Valley reservoirs, Derbyshire   16

3   Into the Dark Peak, Derbyshire   20

4   Bakewell and the Monsal Trail, Derbyshire   24

5   Long Dale and the White Peak, Derbyshire   28

6   Along Rudyard Lake, Staffordshire   32

7   The Staffordshire Moorlands, Staffordshire   36

8   Middleton Top and the High Peak Trail, Derbyshire   40

9   The Five Pits Trail, Derbyshire   44

10   Along the Manifold, Staffordshire   48

11   Along the Tissington Trail, Derbyshire   52

12   Around Carsington Water, Derbyshire   56

13   The charm of the Churnet, Staffordshire   60

14   Osmaston and Shirley, Derbyshire   64

15   The Shropshire Canal, Staffordshire   68

16   Cannock Chase, Staffordshire   72

17   Along the Ashby Woulds Heritage Trail, Leicestershire   76

18   Around Rutland Water, Rutland   80

19   The Silkin Way to Ironbridge, Shropshire   84

20   The Staffordshire & Worcestershire Canal, West Midlands   88

21   Foxton Locks and the Grand Union Canal, Leicestershire   92

22   Through the Teme Valley, Shropshire   96

23   Baddesley Clinton and Packwood House, Warwickshire   100

24   Around Pitsford Water, Northamptonshire   104

25   Stratford Greenway, Warwickshire   108

Acknowledgements   112

Locator map

Huddersfield

Oldham ·Barnsley

MANCHESTER ①

Glossop

·Stockport ②

③ **PEAK DISTRICT**

·Knutsford

·Macclesfield Buxton

④ **Bakewell Matlock** Chesterfield

·Congleton ⑤

Crewe Kidsgrove ⑥ ·Leek ⑦

·Nantwich **STOKE-** ⑩ ⑪ ⑫

Newcastle- **ON-TRENT**

under-Lyme ⑬ ⑭

·Stone Uttoxeter **DERBY**

Market Drayton

·Newport ⑮ ·Stafford

Shrewsbury ·Cannock ⑯ ·Rugeley

·Telford ⑲ ·Lichfield ⑰

WOLVERHAMPTON ·Walsall

·Bridgnorth ⑳ **Nuneaton**

·Dudley **BIRMINGHAM** Hinckley

·Stourbridge

Kidderminster ·Halesowen **COVENTRY** Rugby

⑫② Ludlow Bromsgrove ㉓ **Leamington Spa**

Leominster ·Redditch Warwick ㉔

·Worcester ㉕ Stratford-upon-Avon

Great Malvern Evesham Banbury

Rotherham

SHEFFIELD

⑧ ⑨ **Mansfield**

Alfreton

Ashbourne Ilkeston

Long Eaton **NOTTINGHAM**

Burton upon Trent Loughborough

Melton Mowbray

Oakham ⑱

LEICESTER

Wigston

㉑ Corby

Market Harborough

Kettering

Daventry **Northampton**

Towcester

① **Cycle Ride start point**

–N–

0   20 miles

0   30 km

Introduction to the Peak District & the Heart of England

The Peak District covers a surprising variety of landscapes with many hills and wildlife-filled dales to explore, as well as reservoirs, lakes and railway tracks, which make pleasant and easygoing cycle routes. The waterside rides in this book include the Derwent Valley Reservoirs, Rudyard Lake and Carsington Water and those on easy former railway lines include the Churnet Valley line. There is a designated cycle route in the shape of the family-friendly Tissington Trail. The Heart of England covers a large geographic area taking in the counties of Derbyshire, Leicestershire, Rutland, Shropshire, Staffordshire and Warwickshire. For some, this area may bring to mind images of the industrial heart of the country and indeed, many routes pass through areas which were once home to heavy industry. However, much regeneration has taken place in recent years. What were once railways carrying raw materials are now pleasant, family-friendly cycle tracks, and former sand and gravel pits have been filled with water to create lakes attracting both birdlife and water

sports enthusiasts. Derbyshire's Five Pits Trail follows an undulating route between former coal mines where reclamation and conservation efforts over the last 30 years have seen spoil tips and wasteland gradually replaced by rich hay meadows and maturing woodland. The areas of water here attract upwards of 200 species of bird.

Many of our cycle routes have historic interest. Historic buildings to visit along the way include Castle Howard and the Cistercian Rievaulx Abbey. You could spend days exploring Britain's industrial heritage in Coalbrookdale, now a UNESCO World Heritage Site, which was once the foremost industrial area in the world. This area has several museums which you can stop off at, during or after your cycle ride, or if the weather lets you down.

Many routes follow official, off-road (and therefore traffic-free) tracks. The Pennine Bridleway in Derbyshire and the Stratford Greenway are just a couple of examples of these. Several routes take you past or around bustling towns such as Stratford-upon-Avon or Bakewell, famous for its puddings, and in case you have forgotten, this region is well known as Shakespeare country. Lovers of all things literary will be delighted to know that it is is possible to cycle around the quiet country lanes where the Bard grew up and survey the Grammar School where he is thought to have been educated.

Each cycle ride has a family-friendly pub on, or easily accessible from, the route.

Below: Barton-on-the-Heath, Warwickshire

Using this book

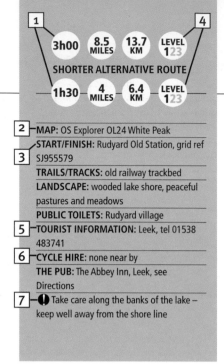

Each cycle ride has a panel giving essential information for the cyclist, including the distance, terrain, nature of the paths, nearest public toilets and cycle hire.

3h00   **8.5 MILES**   **13.7 KM**   **LEVEL 1**23

SHORTER ALTERNATIVE ROUTE

1h30 — **4 MILES**   **6.4 KM**   **LEVEL 1**23

MAP: OS Explorer OL24 White Peak

START/FINISH: Rudyard Old Station, grid ref SJ955579

TRAILS/TRACKS: old railway trackbed

LANDSCAPE: wooded lake shore, peaceful pastures and meadows

PUBLIC TOILETS: Rudyard village

TOURIST INFORMATION: Leek, tel 01538 483741

CYCLE HIRE: none near by

THE PUB: The Abbey Inn, Leek, see Directions

🛈 Take care along the banks of the lake – keep well away from the shore line

1 **MINIMUM TIME:** The time stated for completing each ride is the estimated minimum time that a reasonably fit family group of cyclists would take to complete the circuit. This does not allow for rest or refreshment stops.

2 **MAPS:** Each route is shown on a detailed map. However, some detail is lost because of the restrictions imposed by scale, so for this reason, we recommend that you use the maps in conjunction with a more detailed Ordnance Survey map. The relevant Ordnance Survey Explorer map appropriate for each cycle ride is listed.

3 **START/FINISH:** Here we indicate the start location and parking area. There is a six-figure grid reference prefixed by two letters showing which 100km square of the National Grid it refers to. You'll find more information on grid references on most Ordnance Survey maps.

4 **LEVEL OF DIFFICULTY:** The cycle rides have been graded simply (1 to 3) to give an indication of their relative difficulty. Easier routes, such as those with little total ascent, on easy footpaths or level trails, or those covering shorter distances are graded 1. The hardest routes, either because they include a lot of ascent,

greater distances, or are in hilly, more demanding terrains, are graded 3.

5 **TOURIST INFORMATION:** The nearest tourist information office and contact number is given for further local information, in particular opening details for the attractions listed in the 'Where to go from here' section.

6 **CYCLE HIRE:** We list, within reason, the nearest cycle hire shop/centre.

7 🛈 Here we highlight any potential difficulties or dangers along the route. At a glance you will know if the route is steep or crosses difficult terrain, or if a cycle ride is hilly, encounters a main road, or whether a mountain bike is essential for the off-road trails. If a particular cycle route is thought suitable only for older, fitter children we say so here.

About the pubs

Generally, all the pubs featured are on the cycle route. Some are close to the start/finish point, others are at the midway point, and occasionally, the recommended pub is a short drive from the start/finish point. We have included a cross-section of pubs, from homely village locals and isolated rural gems to traditional inns and upmarket country pubs which specialise in food. What they all have in common is that they serve food and welcome children.

The description of the pub is intended to convey its history and character and in the 'food' section we list a selection of dishes, which indicate the style of food available. Under 'family facilities', we say if the pub offers a children's menu or smaller portions of adult dishes, and whether the pub has a family room, high chairs, baby-changing facilities, or toys. There is detail on the garden, terrace, and any play area.

DIRECTIONS: If the pub is very close to the start point we say see Getting to the Start. If the pub is on the route the relevant direction/map location number is given, in addition to general directions. In some cases the pub is a short drive away from the finish point, so we give detailed directions to the pub from the end of the route.

PARKING: The number of parking spaces is given. All but a few of the cycle rides start away from the pub. If the pub car park is the parking/start point, then we have been given permission by the landlord to print the fact. You should always let the landlord or a member of staff know that you are using the car park before setting off.

OPEN: If the pub is open all week we state 'daily' and if it's open throughout the day we say 'all day', otherwise we just give the days/sessions the pub is closed.

FOOD: If the pub serves food every day, all week we state 'daily' and if food is served throughout the day we say 'all day', otherwise we just give the days/sessions when food is not served.

BREWERY/COMPANY: This is the name of the brewery to which the pub is tied or the pub company that owns it. 'Free house' means the pub is independently owned.

REAL ALE: We list the regular real ales available on handpump. 'Guest beers' indicates that the pub rotates beers from a number of microbreweries.

ROOMS: We list the number of bedrooms and how many are en suite. For prices please call the pub.

Please note that pubs change hands frequently and new chefs are often employed, so menu details and facilities may change at short notice. Not all the pubs featured in this guide are listed in the *AA Pub Guide*. For information on those that are, including AA-rated accommodation, and for a comprehensive selection of pubs across Britain, please refer to the *AA Pub Guide* or see the AA's website www.theAA.com

Alternative refreshment stops

At a glance you will see if there are other pubs or cafés along the route. If there are no other places on the route, we list the nearest village or town where you can find somewhere else to eat and drink.

☛ Where to go from here

Many of the routes are short and may only take a few hours. You may wish to explore the surrounding area after lunch or before tackling the ride, so we have selected a few attractions with children in mind.

Cycling in safety

CYCLING

Cycling is a fun activity which children love, and teaching your child to ride a bike and going on family cycling trips are rewarding experiences. Not only is cycling a great way to travel, but as a regular form of exercise it can make an invaluable contribution to a child's health and fitness, and increase their confidence and sense of independence.

However, the growth of motor traffic has made Britain's roads increasingly dangerous and unattractive to cyclists. Cycling with children is an added responsibility and, as with everything, there is a risk when taking them out for a day's cycling. In recent years many measures have been taken to address this, including the on-going development of the National Cycle Network (8,000 miles utilising quiet lanes and traffic-free paths) and local designated off-road routes for families, such as converted railway lines, canal towpaths and forest tracks.

In devising the cycle rides in this guide, every effort has been made to use these designated cycle paths, or to link them with quiet country lanes and waymarked byways and bridleways. Unavoidably, in a few cases, some relatively busy B-roads have been used to link the quieter, more attractive routes.

Rules of the road

- Ride in single file on narrow and busy roads.
- Be alert, look and listen for traffic, especially on narrow lanes and blind bends and be extra careful when descending steep hills, as loose gravel can lead to an accident.
- In wet weather make sure you keep a good distance between you and other riders.
- Make sure you indicate your intentions clearly.
- Brush up on *The Highway Code* before venturing out on to the road.

Off-road safety code of conduct

- Only ride where you know it is legal to do so. It is forbidden to cycle on public footpaths, marked in yellow. The only 'rights of way' open to cyclists are bridleways (blue markers) and unsurfaced tracks, known as byways, which are open to all traffic and waymarked in red.
- Canal towpaths: you need a permit to cycle on some stretches of towpath (www.waterscape.com). Remember that access paths can be steep and slippery and always get off and push your bike under low bridges and by locks.
- Always yield to walkers and horses, giving adequate warning of your approach.
- Don't expect to cycle at high speeds.
- Keep to the main trail to avoid any unnecessary erosion to the area beside the trail and to prevent skidding, especially if it is wet.
- Remember the Country Code.

Cycling with children

Children can use a child seat from the age of eight months, or from the time they can hold themselves upright. There are a number of child seats available which fit on the front or rear of a bike and towable two-seat trailers are worth investigating. 'Trailer bicycles', suitable for five- to ten-year-olds, can be attached to the rear of an adult's bike, so that the adult has control, allowing the child to pedal if he/she wishes. Family cycling can be made easier by using a tandem, as it can carry a child seat and tow trailers. 'Kiddy-cranks' for shorter legs can be fitted to the rear seat tube, enabling either parent to take their child out cycling. With older children it is better to purchase the right size bike rather than one that is too big, as an oversized bike will be difficult to control, and potentially dangerous.

Preparing your bicycle

A basic routine includes checking the wheels for broken spokes or excess play in the bearings, and checking the tyres for punctures, undue wear and the correct tyre pressures. Ensure that the brake blocks are firmly in place and not worn, and that cables are not frayed or too slack. Lubricate hubs, pedals, gear mechanisms and cables. Make sure you have a pump, a bell, a rear rack to carry panniers and, if cycling at night, a set of working lights.

Preparing yourself

Equipping the family with cycling clothing need not be an expensive exercise. Comfort is the key when considering what to wear. Essential items for well-being on a bike are padded cycling shorts, warm stretch leggings (avoid tight-fitting and seamed trousers like jeans or baggy tracksuit trousers that may become caught in the chain), stiff-soled training shoes, and a wind and waterproof jacket. Fingerless gloves will add to your comfort.

A cycling helmet provides essential protection if you fall off your bike, so they are particularly recommended for young children learning to cycle.

Wrap your child up with several layers in colder weather. Make sure you and those with you are easily visible by car drivers and other road users, by wearing light-coloured or luminous clothing in daylight and reflective strips or sashes in failing light and when it is dark.

What to take with you

Invest in a pair of medium-sized panniers (rucksacks are unwieldy and can affect balance) to carry the necessary gear for you and your family for the day. Take extra clothes with you, the amount depending on the season, and always pack a light wind/waterproof jacket. Carry a basic tool kit (tyre levers, adjustable spanner, a small screwdriver, puncture repair kit, a set of Allen keys) and practical spares, such as an inner tube, a universal brake/gear cable, and a selection of nuts and bolts. Also, always take a pump and a strong lock.

Cycling, especially in hilly terrain and off-road, saps energy, so take enough food and drink for your outing. Always carry plenty of water, especially in hot and humid weather conditions. Consume high-energy snacks like cereal bars, cake or fruits, eating little and often to combat feeling weak and tired. Remember that children get thirsty (and hungry) much more quickly than adults so always have food and diluted juices available for them.

And finally, the most important advice of all—enjoy yourselves!

The jaws of Longdendale

The former Woodhead railway is the spine of a route that also includes reservoir roads amid the impressive scenery of Longdendale.

Rare mammals and UFOs

During the winter you may be lucky enough to see one of Britain's rarest mammals near Crowden. Unlike its lowland cousin, the mountain hare changes the colour of its coat during the winter. Gone is the familiar brown, its place taken by a coat of white fur. With a white coat and potentially several weeks, if not months, of snow, it is difficult to spot these creatures, and thus they escape the attention of predators. In spring the fur gradually moults and is replaced by the familiar brown coat giving the hares an unusual mottled look.

If cycling at dusk, keep an eye on the sky for the 'Longdendale Lights'. Mysterious lights in the sky have been reported here for decades, and the area is a favourite with British UFO spotters.

The lights may be those of aircraft turning over a beacon en route to Manchester airport, or even will-o'-the-wisps – phosphorescent lights resulting from the combustion of natural gases.

the ride

1 From the car park, walk your bicycle the short distance up to the **Longdendale Trail** and turn left. At this initial stage you're passing through immature woodland, one of an innovative series of 'Life for a Life' plantations in the Greater Manchester area, where a departed loved one can be commemorated by the planting of a tree. The tree-lined route passes largely out of sight of **Torside Reservoir**, a popular venue for dinghy sailing, to reach the site of **Crowden Station**.

2 The two houses here are all that remain of the former railway, which was lifted amid great protest in the 1980s. Splendid views now open out up Longdendale, while above the far end of the dam is the little **Chapel of Ease**, **St James' Church**, where the victims of accidents and disease who died during the construction of the railway and reservoirs in the 1840s are buried in unmarked graves. The trackbed continues its easy, gentle climb eastwards just above the shoreline of **Woodhead Reservoir**.

3 This top reservoir narrows to a feeder stream, the infant **River Etherow**. Some miles downstream in **Stockport**, this combines with the rivers **Goyt** and **Tame** to form the **River Mersey**. The end of the line is reached at the **Woodhead Tunnels**. The latest, post-war bore was the last to be used by locomotives. The two earlier ones to the left are of a smaller diameter; one of them still has a narrow gauge railway disappearing into its depths. This allows engineers to service the power cables that have been routed beneath the **Pennines** here. High above, the notorious **Woodhead Pass Road** snakes across the hills. Time for a rest here before returning along the old

Torside Reservoir is popular with water sports enthusiasts as well as cyclists and walkers

3h30	11.5 MILES	18.5 KM	LEVEL 123

SHORTER ALTERNATIVE ROUTE

1h30	6 MILES	9.7 KM	LEVEL 123

MAP: OS Explorer OL1 Dark Peak

START/FINISH: Torside car parking, grid ref SK068999

TRAILS/TRACKS: old railway trackbed, reservoir access roads and tracks

LANDSCAPE: moorland valley with reservoirs and industrial heritage

PUBLIC TOILETS: at start

TOURIST INFORMATION: Glossop, tel 01457 855920

CYCLE HIRE: Longdendale Valley Cycles, Hadfield tel 01457 854672

THE PUB: The Queen's Arms, 1 Shepley Street, Old Glossop

🔵 Don't do this ride on a cold, wet day with an easterly wind, as this will be funnelled down the valley making riding unpleasant and difficult

railway. To your left are steep, heather-clad moors that are home to red grouse.

4 Returning to **Torside** you've completed 6 miles (9.7km). There's plenty more opportunity to the west however, so continue along the **Longdendale Trail** to a road crossing above the dam of **Torside Reservoir**. Take care crossing here. This is also where the **Pennine Way**, England's premier long-distance walk, is crossed. Pass high above **Rhodeswood Reservoir**, with views across to old hillside quarries now reclaimed by juniper woods. In about 0.75 mile (1.2km) reach a fingerpost giving a choice of routes. Turn right here (signed TPT West), go through a bridlegate and down a steep, gravelly path to a lane. Carefully cross this and take the even steeper rough track ahead (wheel your bikes here), leading to an undulating rough lane that eventually reaches the dam holding back **Valehouse Reservoir**. Cross this.

5 At the far side is a service road on the right. This is also a concessionary bridleway, so go through the gates and trace this level, tarred lane alongside the reservoir. As you ride along, the waters will often be obscured by extremely pleasant woodlands. Beyond the lodge house the lane steepens around a series of bends to reach the next dam.

6 Cross this, **Rhodeswood Dam**, to a gate on the left signed for the **Longdendale Trail**. This steep track rises to an open gateway where you turn right up a narrower track to a bridlegate on the left. Take this to access the trackbed and turn left to return to the start of the ride.

Getting to the start

Torside car park is on the B6105 south of Torside Reservoir to the east of Manchester. From the A628, turn right on to the B6105 just past Crowden.

Why do this cycle ride?

In this great trough-like valley that cuts through the Dark Peak, a string of reservoirs were developed during Victorian times to supply Manchester with water. The route follows a reclaimed railway along the shores of the reservoirs, while a branch crosses one of the dams to incorporate a pleasant wooded waterside stretch.

Researched and written by: Neil Coates

Longdendale **DERBYSHIRE**

Longdendale DERBYSHIRE

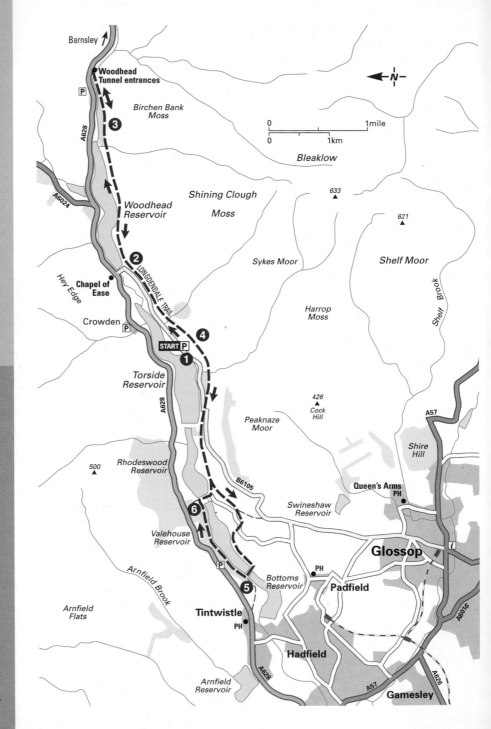

Barnsley

Woodhead
Tunnel entrances

P

A628

3

Birchen Bank
Moss

0   1mile
0   1km

Bleaklow

633 ▲

621 ▲

A6024

*Woodhead
Reservoir*

*Shining Clough
Moss*

Shelf Moor

2

LONGDENDALE TRAIL

Sykes Moor

Shelf Brook

Hey Edge

**Chapel of
Ease**

Crowden

P

*Harrop
Moss*

4

START P

1

A57

*Torside
Reservoir*

A628

426 ▲
*Cock
Hill*

*Peaknaze
Moor*

*Shire
Hill*

500 ▲

*Rhodeswood
Reservoir*

B6105

Queen's Arms
PH ●

6

*Swineshaw
Reservoir*

Glossop

i

*Valehouse
Reservoir*

A6016

Arnfield Brook

P

PH ●

Padfield

*Bottoms
Reservoir*

5

*Arnfield
Flats*

Tintwistle

PH ●

Hadfield

*Arnfield
Reservoir*

A628

A57

A626

Gamesley

The Queen's Arms

At the heart of a web of back lanes and passages that wind between the church, village cross and the nearby Manor Park, this is a splendid little pub in the picture-postcard village of Old Glossop. Hemmed in by fine old gritstone cottages, it's a solid street corner local with climbing roses and hanging baskets adding a splash of colour to the light stone exterior. The small taproom oozes character with darkwood panelling, deep upholstered wall benches, sporting prints on the walls, and eye-catching leaded glass windows. The low-beamed and carpeted L-shaped main bar is primarily laid up for dining, although drinkers are welcome here. There is a great range of real ales with a changing guest beer.

about the pub

The Queen's Arms
1 Shepley Street, Old Glossop
Derbyshire SK13 7RZ
Tel 01457 862451

DIRECTIONS: The Queen's Arms is about 4 miles (6.4km) from Torside Car Park. Load the bikes on the car and turn left out of the car park on to the B6105 towards Glossop. In about 3 miles (4.8km), on a long downhill stretch into the outskirts of Glossop, pass the turn for the cemetery (right) and shortly turn left into Church Street. Pass the church, then bend right, and downhill, to find the pub on the left at a junction

PARKING: good on-street parking

OPEN: daily, all day

FOOD: daily, all day

BREWERY/COMPANY: Punch Taverns

REAL ALE: Black Sheep Bitter, Worthington, Pedigree and Unicorn, guest beer

Food

Expect to find a standard printed menu listing pub favourites – roast chicken, gammon, steak and kidney pie – and an ever-changing blackboard listing the likes of braised steak, lamb Henry and vegetable lasagne. Good value Sunday lunches; separate restaurant menu.

Family facilities

Although facilities are limited for children they are welcome away from the bar and a basic children's menu is available. Outdoor seating is limited.

Alternative refreshment stops

There is a part-time snack bar at Torside Visitor Centre.

☞ Where to go from here

In Stockport town centre are the fascinating Air Raid Shelters, a warren of tunnels hewn into the sandstone cliffs above the Mersey into which the townsfolk and millworkers could retreat during the Blitz (www.stockport.gov.uk and follow the links in Leisure and Culture).

Longdendale DERBYSHIRE

15

The Upper Derwent Valley reservoirs

A long and challenging route around the stunning chain of reservoirs in the Upper Derwent Valley.

Birds and bouncing bombs

Many of the high moorlands throughout the northern area of the Peak District are managed for grouse shooting, a long-established practice dating from Victorian times. In today's more conservation-minded days, the gamekeepers employed by the great estates and landowning companies are much more sympathetic to the natural predators of these game birds than were their predecessors.

Nonetheless, birds of prey such as the peregrine falcon are still targeted both by unscrupulous keepers and egg collectors, so defensive measures and management techniques are now in place in order to protect such raptors. You may see a peregrine 'stooping' (diving) at up to 150mph to kill its prey on the wing. A much more rare bird of prey is also regaining a toe-hold in the woods around the Upper Derwent reservoirs – the goshawk has recently been reintroduced, and is breeding successfully. During the nesting season (April to June), a remote-controlled camera sends back live pictures of a goshawk nest to the visitor centre at Fairholmes.

Paintings in the Yorkshire Bridge Inn are a reminder that the 617 Dambusters Squadron trained with their bouncing bombs here on Derwent and Howden reservoirs before their remarkable raid on the Ruhr dams in 1943. This was also the location of the film made in 1954 which tells the story of the raid.

the ride

1 Except on summer Sundays, the initial stage of the route is shared with cars, so take care. Head north from the **Fairholmes Centre**, rising to the level of the dam top of Derwent Reservoir. This dam was started in 1902, a year after the dam at Howden. Easy cycling with great views takes you past the memorial to Tip, who was a sheepdog who kept vigil beside his master's body, after the master perished on Howden Moors.

2 Dipping in and out of **Ouzelden Clough**, the road passes close to the site of **Birchinlee**, or 'Tin Town'. This village was created to house the workers who constructed the dams. Most of the buildings were of corrugated iron, hence the nickname. There's little evidence of the place today. Passing beside **Howden Dam**, the route now circuits a long arm of **Howden Reservoir** to arrive at the turning circle at Kings Tree, the end of the tarred road. This is a good place to turn around (9 mile/14.5km round trip) as the next section is more challenging.

3 Beyond the gate the route becomes a rough forest road that climbs gently through the woods above the narrowing tip of Howden Reservoir. At a fork keep right to drop to the old packhorse bridge at **Slippery Stones**. This bridge originally spanned the River Derwent at the hamlet of Derwent, now drowned beneath the waters of Ladybower Reservoir. The structure was rebuilt at this lonely spot on the Howden Moors in the 1940s. Just above the bridge swing sharp right to climb the roughening track along the eastern shore of the reservoir.

Howden Dam

4h00 **15 MILES** **24.2 KM** **LEVEL 1 2 3**

SHORTER ALTERNATIVE ROUTE

2h30 **9 MILES** **14.5 KM** **LEVEL 1 2 3**

MAP: OS Explorer OL1 Dark Peak

START/FINISH: Fairholmes Visitor Centre, Upper Derwent Valley, grid ref SK176894

TRAILS/TRACKS: tarred lanes and rough mountain roads

LANDSCAPE: woodland and lakes amidst moorland and craggy valleys

PUBLIC TOILETS: at start

TOURIST INFORMATION: Fairholmes, tel 01433 650953

CYCLE HIRE: Fairholmes, tel 01433 651261

THE PUB: Yorkshire Bridge Inn, Ashopton Road, Bamford

🚲 Take care at the start along a road shared by cars. There are rough tracks on the longer ride. The complete ride is suitable for older family groups using mountain or hybrid-style bikes

Getting to the start

Start at the Fairholmes Visitor Centre in the Upper Derwent Valley. This is signposted off the A57 Glossop to Sheffield road, immediately west of Ashopton Viaduct, which crosses the north arm of Ladybower Reservoir. Fairholmes is 2 miles (3.2km) along this minor road.

Why do this cycle ride?

This route takes full advantage of the contrasting landscapes of the northern part of the National Park. It's a challenging family route of two halves: a gentle, forested, tarred lane replaced by rough upland tracks.

Researched and written by: Neil Coates

4 The going is pretty rough for a mile (1.6km) or so before a well-graded service road heralds the approach to **Howden Dam**, particularly colourful in late spring and early summer when the rhododendrons are in full flower. A steep, rougher descent follows before the route comes close to the reservoir edge where steep, grassy banks drop straight into the water, so take care here. The track improves considerably as the route nears **Derwent Dam**. Passing close to one of the towers, the way develops into a tarred lane and passes the first of some isolated houses.

5 You can cut short the ride by turning right to pass the foot of **Derwent Dam** to return to **Fairholmes** (9.5 miles/15.2km). The main route continues south past **St Henry's Chapel**, becoming rougher again as it rounds an inlet to an interpretation board describing the now-lost village of Derwent which stood here until the 1940s.

6 Reaching a gateway, join the tarred lane and drop to the main road. Turn right along the wide cycle path across **Ashopton Viaduct**, and right again at the far end.

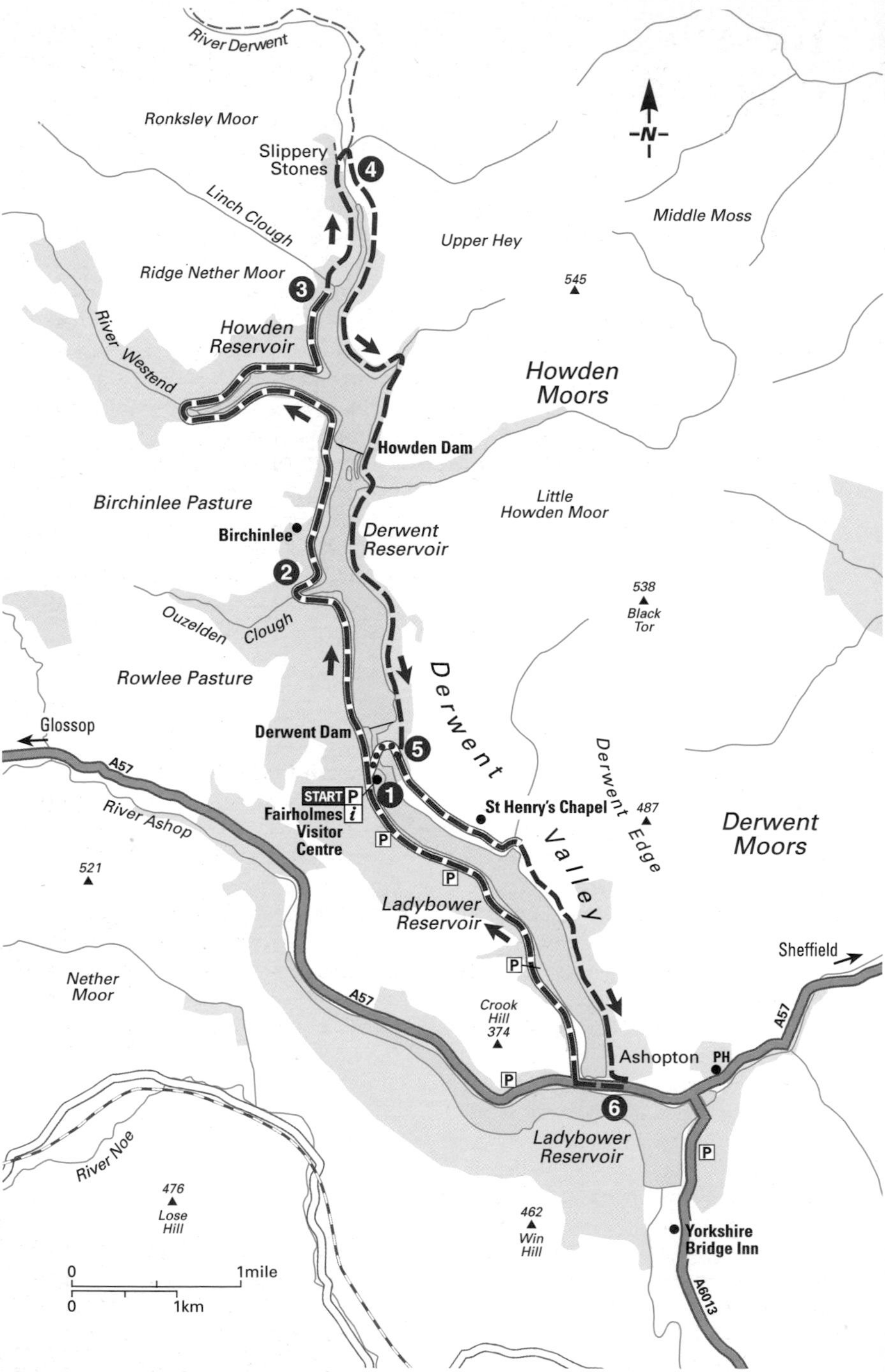

River Derwent

Ronksley Moor

Slippery
Stones ④

Linch Clough

Upper Hey

Middle Moss

-N-

Ridge Nether Moor ③

Howden
Reservoir

545 ▲

Howden
Moors

River Westend

Howden Dam

Birchinlee Pasture

Birchinlee ●

②

Ouzelden Clough

Rowlee Pasture

Derwent
Reservoir

Little
Howden Moor

538
▲
Black
Tor

Glossop

A57

River Ashop

521
▲

Nether
Moor

Derwent Dam

START P
Fairholmes i
Visitor
Centre

P

⑤

①

P

St Henry's Chapel ●

487
▲

Derwent

Valley

Derwent Edge

Derwent
Moors

A57

Ladybower
Reservoir

Crook
Hill
374
▲

P

P

P

Ashopton ●

Sheffield

A57

PH ●

River Noe

476
▲
Lose
Hill

462
▲
Win
Hill

⑥

Ladybower
Reservoir

P

● Yorkshire
Bridge Inn

A6013

0 _____ 1mile
0 _____ 1km

Yorkshire Bridge Inn

An armful of awards have been handed out to 'The Bridge' in recent years, not least third place in Pub Garden of the Year. The 200-year-old pub nestles in close to the famous Ladybower Reservoir, scene of the Dambusters' training exercises before their dramatic raid. In summer you'll want to make use of the courtyard and beer garden, while in more inclement weather the bars provide a cosy sanctuary and plenty of interest. Comfortable rooms sport open fires or wood-burning stoves and low beams hung with tankards and jars; one displays photographs of long-lost villages (now under the reservoirs), while another remembers the Dambusters raid.

about the pub

Yorkshire Bridge Inn
Ashopton Road, Bamford
Hope Valley, Derbyshire S33 0AZ
Tel 01433 651361
www.yorkshire-bridge.co.uk

DIRECTIONS: the Yorkshire Bridge Inn is about 3 miles (4.8km) from the Fairholmes car park. Return to the main road and turn left across the viaduct. At the traffic lights turn right towards Bamford; the pub is 1 mile (1.6km) on the right

PARKING: 60

OPEN: daily, all day

FOOD: daily, all day Sunday

BREWERY/COMPANY: free house

REAL ALE: Black Sheep Bitter, Theakston's Old Peculier, Copper Dragon, IPA, Challenger

ROOMS: 14 en suite

Food

Food is available in the bar and dining room and starters can range from garlic mushrooms to giant Yorkshire puddings. Main courses are equally varied with dishes such as chicken Italiano, giant prawn cocktail or, from the specials menu, rosemary and garlic lamb steak with caramelised onion and redcurrant sauce or chicken Florentine. An impressive selection of sandwiches, filled jacket potatoes and salad platters will more than satisfy.

Family facilities

Children are made very welcome in the bars and the fascinating memorabilia should keep them entertained. On sunny days there's no better place to be than in the beautiful, award-winning gardens. Young children have their own menu and there are cycle racks and secure overnight garaging for guests' use.

Alternative refreshment stops

There is a snack bar at Fairholmes Visitor Centre and the Ladybower Inn is near Ashopton Viaduct.

☛ Where to go from here

The various caverns at Castleton are a long-time favourite with visitors of all ages. The most unusual is Speedwell Cavern, where access is by an underground boat trip (www.speedwellcavern.co.uk).

Into the Dark Peak

Explore the Sett Valley Trail before branching off along well-graded back lanes and the Pennine bridleway to the foot of the forbidding Kinder Scout.

Bowden Bridge Quarry

On the extension to the route up the Sett Valley you'll pass by Bowden Bridge Quarry. This commands a special place in the hearts of many ramblers and those who seek open access to England's higher and wilder places. In the 1920s there was a growing demand from people who lived in the towns and cities adjoining what is now the Peak District National Park, for the fresh air and freedom that the hills offered. These areas, the property of the wealthy classes and the preserve of those shooting grouse for a few weeks a year, were fiercely guarded by gamekeepers and staff employed to keep interlopers off these great estates. Minor confrontations and court cases bubbled on until the early 1930s, when things came to a head. On 24th April 1932 several hundred supporters of the 'right to roam' assembled at Bowden Bridge Quarry and set off for the moorlands of Kinder Scout, to assert a right to roam freely. They were soon confronted by estate staff determined to keep them off.

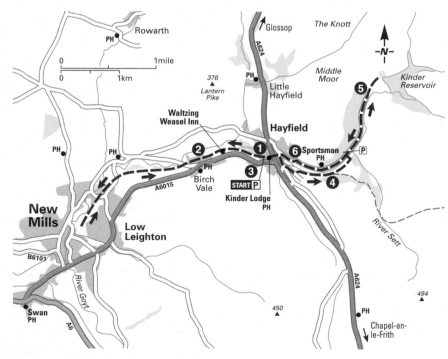

Kinder Downfall at Kinder Scout

| 3h00 | 8.75 MILES | 14.1 KM | LEVEL 123 |

SHORTER ALTERNATIVE ROUTE

| 1h45 | 5 MILES | 8 KM | LEVEL 123 |

MAP: OS Explorer OL1 Dark Peak

START/FINISH: village car park at Hayfield Old Station, grid ref SK037870

TRAILS/TRACKS: old railway trackbed, back lanes. One short footpath link where you walk your bicycle

LANDSCAPE: river valley woodlands with hill views; the extension has superb views to Kinder Scout plateau

PUBLIC TOILETS: Hayfield car park

TOURIST INFORMATION: Hayfield, tel 01663 746222

CYCLE HIRE: Old Station, Hayfield, tel 01663 746222

THE PUB: The Walzing Weasel Inn, Hayfield, just off the route

Getting to the start

Start from the Hayfield village car park signposted off the A624 Glossop to Chapel-en-le-Frith road. Turn on to the A6015 road for New Mills and then turn immediately right just after the Kinder Lodge pub.

Why do this cycle ride?

This simple there-and-back route, ideal for families with young children, passes through the lower Sett Valley. An extension to the route heads towards Kinder Scout along bridlepaths and reservoir roads, revealing excellent views and passing a famous marker along the way.

Researched and written by: Neil Coates

The protest leaders were arrested and jailed. This action, which became known as the Mass Trespass, led to improvements to access to the countryside and to today's national parks' system. On a busy Sunday, maybe 3,000 people would take the trains from Manchester to Hayfield Station to enjoy such hard-won freedoms. There's a plaque on the quarry wall recalling this seminal day.

the ride

1 The first stage is an easy ride along the trackbed of the former Hayfield to New Mills railway line that closed in the 1960s. Head away from the information and toilet block, following **'Sett Valley Trail'** signs past the cycle hire centre. Once through a gateway a long, gentle descent takes the ride through the mature woodlands lining the old railway line. One section is a nature reserve; **Bluebell Wood** hints that a good time to visit is in May.

2 On the right, the mill lodge of one of countless local mills has been transformed into a fishery and is overshadowed by the hill of **Lantern Pike**. The trail bends to a roadside gate; don't take this but turn right to a lower gateway. Carefully cross the main road to the gateway opposite. The trail continues as an easy ride along a wooded course, crossing three more road crossings (all controlled by gates) to arrive abruptly at the end of the line, a gateway into **St George's Road** in **New Mills**. Turn here to retrace the route to the car park, a round trip of 5 miles (8km).

3 To extend the route along the **Sett Valley** and into the National Park, continue through the car park (signposted '**Kinder Trail**') and use the pedestrian-controlled lights to cross over the main road, keeping ahead to find the main village street. Turn right up this to reach the distinctively shaped old toll house near the hill crest. Fork left here, then immediately left again along **Valley Road**, signposted '**No Through Road**'. This quiet lane drops past cottages and houses to trace a course beside the lively **River Sett**. This is also the waymarked route of the new **Pennine Bridleway**.

4 Beyond the last cottages, you'll soon reach a parting of ways. The Pennine Bridleway is signed along a right fork, while a footpath is signed left along a wide path above the river. Dismount here and wheel your bicycle beside the water, shortly passing a footbridge to reach the **Peak Park Ranger Station** and a tarred access road. Pedal along this to **Bowden Bridge Quarry car park**. Turn right along the peaceful tarred lane. This undulates through woodland to arrive at a gateway into a service road to **Kinder Reservoir**. This is a concessionary bridleway, so pass through the gates and continue gently uphill to reach a turning area at the end of the road. It's well worth securing your bikes to rail fencing here and taking the very steep, cobbled bridlepath ahead-left a further 400yds (366m) to enjoy the views to **Kinder Downfall** (seasonal) waterfall and the surrounding hills.

5 Reclaim your bikes and return to **Bowden Bridge car park**. Remain on the lane here, soon passing by the **Sportsman** pub to reach the outskirts of **Hayfield**. The roads are narrow, so take care as you descend past cottages.

6 Ignore the first sharp left turn (**Spring Vale Road**); at the second a very short hill (**Bank Street**) drops you to the village centre. Turn left across the bridge, then right alongside the church to find the crossing back to the car park.

Peaceful Birch Vale, where you will find the Waltzing Weasel Inn

Waltzing Weasel Inn

Set within the heart of the Peak District, this traditional, 200-year-old country inn is popular with walkers and business people alike – no music or machines and no mobile phones permitted. Country antiques, carved oak pews and settles, stripped old tables, Victorian sporting prints, and a huge stone fireplace with roaring log fires in winter are impressive features of the cosy bar, while from the secluded terrace and garden and the mullion-windowed restaurant there are dramatic views of Kinder Scout. It's all very quiet, peaceful and homely, with the added attractions of good beer, decent wines and above average pub food.

Food

A solidly English bar menu is supplemented by daily dishes such as sardine tapenade, stir-fried vegetable crepes and smoked Loch Fyne salmon. You'll find sandwiches, home-made soups, freshly baked pizzas, Peak pie and fish of the day, and there's always a hearty stew or casserole. There is a good range of vegetarian meals plus a set evening menu in the restaurant and popular traditional Sunday roast lunches.

about the pub

Waltzing Weasel Inn
New Mills Road, Birch Vale
High Peak, Derbyshire SK22 1BT
Tel 01663 743402
www.w-weasel.co.uk

DIRECTIONS: 0.5 miles (800m) from Hayfield along the A6015 towards New Mills
PARKING: 42
OPEN: daily
FOOD: daily
BREWERY/COMPANY: free house
REAL ALE: Marston's Best, Pedigree, Timothy Taylor Landlord, Greene King IPA
ROOMS: 5 en suite

Family facilities

Although there are no specific facilities for children they are welcome inside the pub and small portions of most main dishes are available. From the enclosed patio garden to the side there are good views for summer eating and drinking.

Alternative refreshment stops

There are plenty of pubs, cafés and restaurants in Hayfield.

☛ Where to go from here

The Chestnut Centre Wildlife Park near Chapel-en-le-Frith specialises in rare mammals and birds, such as otters and owls, from Britain, Europe and beyond (www.ottersandowls.co.uk).

Bakewell and the Monsal Trail

An easy ride from the town of Bakewell, with its railway heritage, which loops through a picturesque limestone village and riverside hay meadows.

Bakewell and the Monsal Trail

The Monsal Trail is largely the trackbed of the former main line railway linking Manchester Central to Derby and London St Pancras. Opened in 1849 and built by the Midland Railway, it was latterly renowned for its comfortable Pullman carriages before closing in 1969. There

Bakewell is famed for its puddings, but there's much more to look out for here, including the Old House Museum and the lively market (Wednesdays are particularly busy and vibrant). Great Longstone was once a renowned centre for stocking manufacture, established by immigrant Flemish weavers who often traded their goods at the village market cross.

the ride

1 Access to the trackbed remains via the gap at the left side of the imposing structure. Turn left along the level track, a compacted and well-surfaced route that, beyond the industrial units that occupy the

are ambitious plans to restore services through the Peak District, and a start has been made at nearby Rowsley, from where Peak Rail runs seasonal services through to Matlock and the surviving branch line to Derby. During the summer months the railway's banks (and the roadside verges) are bright with the vivid blue flower of the meadow cranesbill, that can often be seen in great drifts along with the ox-eye daisies and willowherb.

former goods yard, runs initially through thin woods. Passing beneath the main road, the buildings of Bakewell are left behind and soon **Hassop Old Station** comes into view.

2 The station buildings are largely gone, although an old warehouse has been converted to other uses. Beyond here, the trees become less constricting, and views to the hill slopes climbing towards **Longstone Edge** draw the eye. There's an

Right: A medieval cross on the small green of the limestone-built village of Great Longstone

3h00	8 MILES	12.9 KM	LEVEL 1 2 3

SHORTER ALTERNATIVE ROUTE

1h15	5.25 MILES	8.4 KM	LEVEL 1 2 3

MAP: OS Explorer OL24 White Peak

START/FINISH: Bakewell Old Station, grid ref SK223690

TRAILS/TRACKS: old railway trackbed and back lanes

LANDSCAPE: woods and pastures below limestone edges, river valley, hay meadows

PUBLIC TOILETS: central Bakewell

TOURIST INFORMATION: Bakewell, tel 01629 813227

CYCLE HIRE: none near by

THE PUB: Monsal Head Hotel, Monsal Head

🅘 One short climb, one long downhill stretch

Getting to the start

The old railway station in Bakewell is located on Station Road – the road that forks off to the right at the memorial as you take the A619 road for Baslow out of the town centre and cross the bridge over the Wye. There's ample parking at the old station.

Why do this cycle ride?

This is an easy, largely level ride from Bakewell into the folded, wooded countryside that characterises the eastern fringes of the national park. A couple of shorter add-ons include one of the Peak's charming little villages and a pleasant ride above the Wye Valley.

Researched and written by: Neil Coates

abundance of summer wild flowers along this section. The old trackbed passes under and over several roads and lanes before reaching the impressive buildings at Great Longstone's **old station**. The station partially retains its canopy, while next door is one of the buildings of the Thornbridge Estate.

3 A sign here warns that there is no exit for cycles beyond this point, but it is worth cycling the extra 0.25 mile (400m) to the end of the useable track for some great views across towards the hidden **River Wye** in its deep valley. You can choose here to simply retrace your route back to Bakewell, a total distance of 5.25 miles (8.4km). Another option, though, is to return to **Great Longstone Station** and take the steep flight of steps, left, to a minor road. Turn left along this, an easy, level ride to the village centre at **Great Longstone**.

4 At the market cross and village green, fork right along either of the lanes. Both wind down to the main street, lined with fine limestone cottages and houses, to reach the White Lion. Just beyond this, take **Church Lane**, left, to rise up a gentle hill to the parish **church**. The road bends right here, commencing an undulating, easy ride along this narrow road, **Beggarway Lane**, offering excellent views up to **Longstone Edge** and occasional glimpses back towards Bakewell.

5 In about 0.75 miles (1.2km), turn right along the lane that leaves at a left bend. This, **Longreave Lane**, is an easy downhill

Left: Medieval five-arch bridge spanning the River Wye in Bakewell

Bakewell

DERBYSHIRE

25

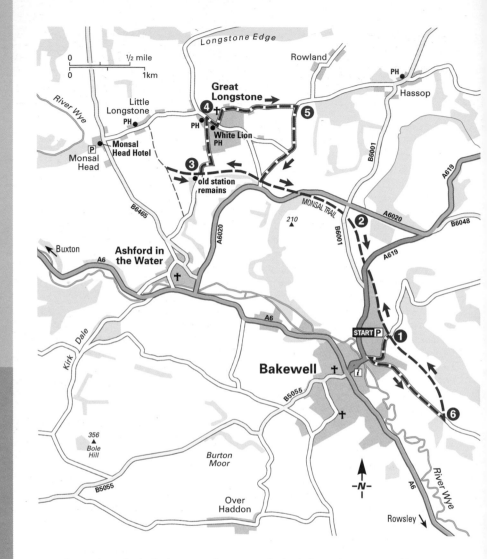

coast for nearly a mile (1.6km), eventually reaching a junction at a railway overbridge. Fork left here just before the bridge, up a gravelly ramp to regain the old railway. Turn left to return to **Bakewell**. To extend the route you can now cycle across the car park and take **Station Road** downhill (take care by the parked cars). At the junction at the bottom turn sharp left along **Coombs Road**, passing the car park entrance. This peaceful, level lane runs for about

a mile (1.6km), amid pastures and hay meadows before reaching a high-arched viaduct crossing.

6 Immediately before the viaduct, look for the **Monsal Trail** board on the left, indicating a short, sharp incline up which you wheel your bicycle to gain the old railway. Turn left to return to **Bakewell**; there are some good views across the town from this elevated route.

Monsal Head Hotel

about the pub

Monsal Head Hotel
Monsal Head, Bakewell
Derbyshire DE45 1NL
Tel 01629 640250
www.monsalhead.com

DIRECTIONS: from Bakewell Old Station drop to the main road junction and turn right for Baslow. In 0.5 miles (800m) fork left (B6001) and continue to a traffic island. Turn left, then right after a mile (1.6km) to Great Longstone. Continue through the village to Monsal Head

PARKING: 15 (pay car park adjacent)

OPEN: daily, all day

FOOD: daily, all day

BREWERY/COMPANY: free house

REAL ALE: Caledonian Deuchars IPA, Theakston Best and Old Peculiar, Timothy Taylor Landlord, local guest beers

ROOMS: 7 en suite

Set against a spectacular backdrop of hills and dales, the disused viaduct at Monsal Head has long been a familiar landmark in the Peak District. In days gone by horses pulled guests and their luggage from the railway station up the steep incline to this imposing, ivy-covered hotel. However, the place for walkers, cyclists and passing trade is the Stables Pub to the rear of the building. The former stables, converted into a thriving bar, offer real ale and great food. Outside it's bare stone, two storeys with a steep pitched roof and wooden sash windows, while inside the fittings have been largely retained, with half-a-dozen stalls converted into individual drinking corners, each with cushioned wall benches. Add a huge solid fuel stove for cold winter days, eight real ales on handpump and a super courtyard garden for summer drinking and you have a great pub to retreat to after your ride.

Food

One menu operates throughout the restaurant, bar and eating area, with meat dishes uch as chicken Hartington and Monsal Wellington, as well as halibut, monkfish, salmon and scallops from a good fishy choice. Local produce is used where possible. Small plates, grills, salads and jacket potatoes extend the range.

Family facilities

Children are welcome away from the bar and small children have their own menu. There's good courtyard seating with plenty of tables and chairs.

Alternative refreshment stops

Pubs in Great Longstone (The Crispin Inn and The White Lion); plenty of choice in Bakewell.

☞ Where to go from here

The Peak Rail preserved railway (south of Rowsley) runs seasonal services, mostly steam operated (www.peakrail.co.uk). The spectacular medieval fortified manor of Haddon Hall has featured in many films and TV programmes (www.haddonhall.co.uk).

Long Dale and the White Peak

From the Tissington Trail on to peaceful backroads near Hartington, returning via Long Dale and the new Pennine Bridleway.

Fossils

The main reason for building the railway on what is now the High Peak Trail was to move limestone from quarries to canals and lowland railways. The line itself burrows through cuttings and across embankments of limestone, and embedded within the limestone you'll find fossils of the creatures that lived in the shallow tropical seas that covered this area 300 million years ago. The most recognisable of these are the remains of crinoids. These were a kind of primitive starfish that attached themselves to rocks by a cord made up of small segments. It is these that you'll find in blocks and slabs of limestone, often in great numbers and looking like the mixed up contents of a necklace box. Belemnites are another fossil that are also found in numbers here. The fossil is that of the shell and looks very like a bullet casing!

On warm and sunny summer days stop for a break in Long Dale and take a close look at the limestone walls, where you may be lucky enough to catch a glimpse of a common lizard basking in the heat. Only about 4in (10cm) long, they're very agile and the slightest movement will see them disappear into the wall crevices and cracks they call home.

the ride

1 From **Parsley Hay** head south along the **High Peak Trail**. The firm, level surface means you can concentrate on the views as much as the way ahead – but look out for walkers and horse riders, as this is a multi-user trail.

2 In a short distance the route forks; keep right here, joining the **Tissington Trail**, the former trackbed of the line down to Ashbourne. Passing through a deep cutting, the trail emerges to reveal good views across towards the Staffordshire Moors. Shortly, to your left, the distinct hill is **Lean Low**, the burial site of our distant forefathers – a tumulus, or burial mound, was found on this windswept summit. The trail sweeps close to **Hartington-moor Farm** before crossing a bridge and reaching the former **Hartington Station**.

3 Take time to explore the site here before continuing south – and start counting the bridges. At the **seventh bridge** – three above you, four that you cross – you need to dismount and wheel your bike down the footpath on the right. There's a **barn** and trees off to the right and an old **quarry** to the left as additional locator points (if you reach the main road on your left you've gone too far). This drops to a quiet lane bound for **Biggin-by-Hartington** and is now your route to the left, a long and very gentle climb between the characteristic walled pastures and hay meadows of this fertile plateau. Cresting a low ridge, splendid views open out across the western Peak District and ahead to **Biggin**.

4 To visit **Biggin** itself you can divert right along **Drury Lane** to find the village shop and the **Waterloo Inn** (to return to the main route just pass by the pub on your right, the main route then comes in from the left at a junction). The main route avoids the village and descends to a couple of sharp bends at **Cotterill Farm** before reaching a junction. Keep ahead here (the village option rejoins here) and go straight through the next junction (pond on the right). An easy, all-but-level stretch ends with a narrow descent down **Harding's Lane** to a junction with the B5054.

5 Take great care crossing here; it's easiest to cycle down the main road a few yards to allow a clear view of traffic before crossing into the lane directly opposite. This is the start of a delightful, easy ascent along the valley floor of **Long Dale**. The lane meanders lazily beneath limestone crags and screes, imperceptibly rising for about 2 miles (3.2km) where a lane joins from the left. Ignore this and keep ahead, passing **Vincent House Farm** to a junction. You can turn right here to return to Parsley Hay, but continuing along the main lane allows you to visit a fine country pub.

6 The lane continues to rise gently, soon leaving the dale behind, unveiling views across the Staffordshire moorlands. Ignore the next turn right and continue to a crossroads at **High Needham**. Here turn right along an undulating road to reach the **Royal Oak** pub at **Hurdlow**, which is adjacent to the **High Peak Trail**. Pick up the Trail beyond the old **railway bridge** and head south to return the last 2 miles (3.2km) to **Parsley Hay**.

3h30 — 12 MILES — 19.3 KM — LEVEL 123

MAP: OS Explorer OL24 White Peak
START/FINISH: Parsley Hay on the High Peak Trail, grid ref SK147637
TRAILS/TRACKS: partly along the High Peak, then Tissington trails and along usually quiet minor roads
LANDSCAPE: the route winds across the limestone plateau of the White Peak and includes an easy ride up a superb, shallow limestone dry-valley
PUBLIC TOILETS: at Parsley Hay
TOURIST INFORMATION: Bakewell, tel 01629 813227
CYCLE HIRE: Derbyshire County Council centre at Parsley Hay, tel 01298 84493 www.derbyshire.gov.uk/countryside
THE PUB: The Royal Oak, Hurdlow, see point 6 on route

One crossing of the B5054 near Hartington requires particular care. Walkers and horse-riders also use the High Peak Trail. Suitable for family groups who have some experience with on-road cycling, best tackled by older children

Getting to the start
Parsley Hay Centre is on the High Peak Trail and is signposted off the A515 Buxton to Ashbourne road. There is a pay car park here.

Why do this cycle ride?
A good mix of railway trackbed and some quiet by-roads that thread between stone villages, make this an easy ride on the White Peak's limestone plateau. With glimpses into some of the deeper dales, your main preoccupation may be in identifying some of the knolls and hills that form a wide horizon, while Long Dale is an enchanting stretch up a valley with wild flowers in the summer.

Researched and written by: Neil Coates

Long Dale DERBYSHIRE

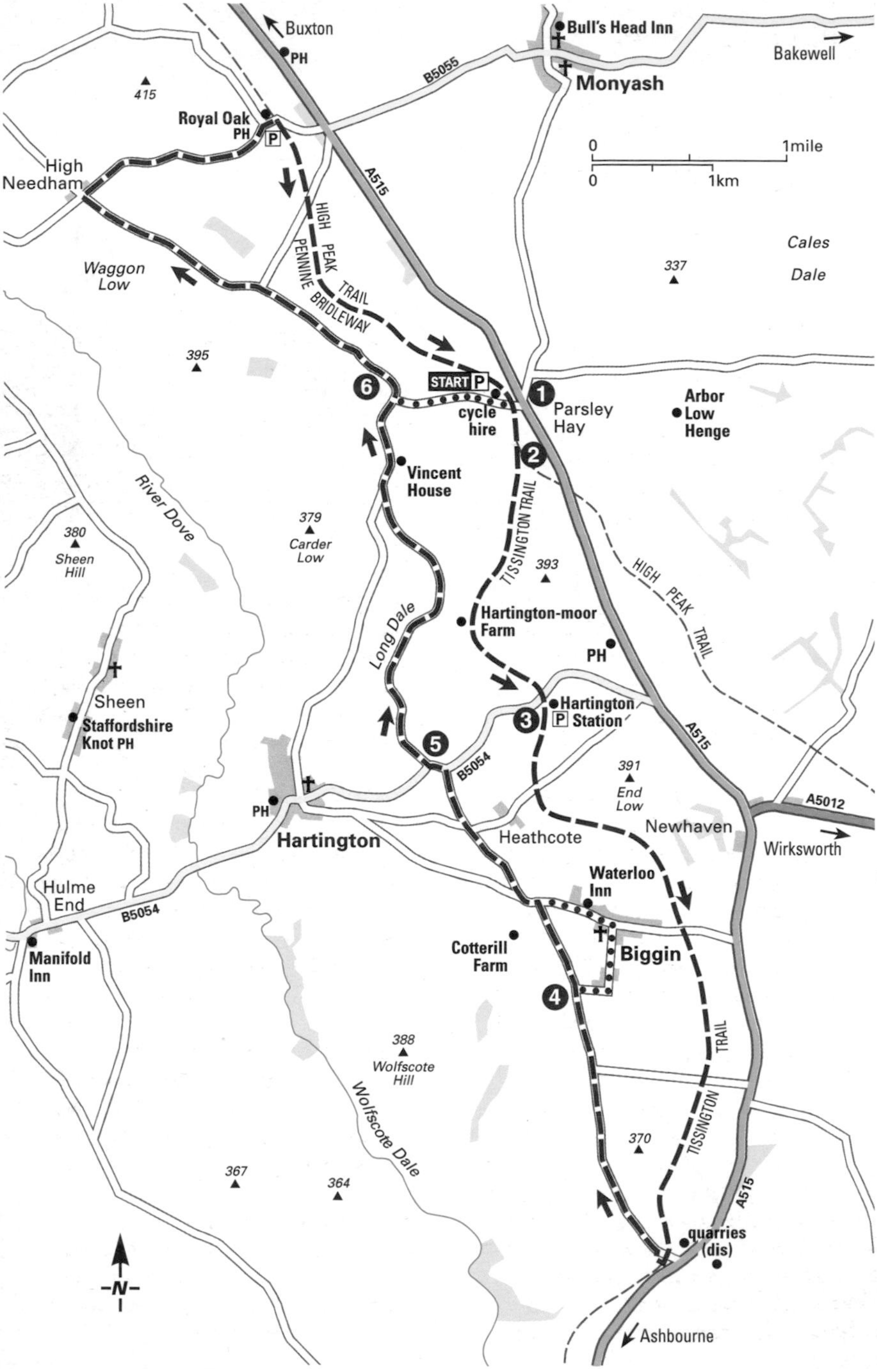

Buxton
PH
Bull's Head Inn
Bakewell
B5055
Monyash

415

Royal Oak
PH
P

High
Needham

Cales
Dale

337

Waggon
Low

HIGH PEAK TRAIL
PENNINE BRIDLEWAY

A515

395

6

START P

cycle
hire

1 Parsley
Hay

Arbor
Low
Henge

0   1mile
0   1km

2

Vincent
House

379
Carder
Low

TISSINGTON TRAIL

393

HIGH PEAK TRAIL

River Dove

380
Sheen
Hill

Long Dale

Hartington-moor
Farm

PH

5

3 Hartington
P Station

Sheen
Staffordshire
Knot PH

B5054

391
End
Low

Newhaven

A5012

Wirksworth

A515

PH

Hartington

Heathcote

Hulme
End
B5054

Waterloo
Inn

Biggin

Manifold
Inn

Cotterill
Farm

4

388
Wolfscote
Hill

TISSINGTON TRAIL

Wolfscote Dale

370

367

364

quarries
(dis)

A515

-N-

Ashbourne

Royal Oak

about the pub

Royal Oak
Hurdlow, Buxton
Derbyshire SK17 9QJ
Tel 01298 83288

DIRECTIONS: from Parsley Hay car park turn
left to the A515. Turn left towards Buxton.
In about 1.75 miles (2.8km) turn left towards
Longnor. The Royal Oak is just across the
railway bridge next to the Hurdlow car park
on the High Peak Trail

PARKING: 30

OPEN: Tuesday to Sunday, all day

FOOD: daily, all day

BREWERY/COMPANY: free house

REAL ALE: Bass, Marston's Pedigree,
guest beer

*Just as it did when it was built some
200 years ago, the Royal Oak continues
to serve railway users, although today it
provides welcome refreshment to weary
walkers and cyclists tackling the High
Peak Trail, a 17-mile (27km) route that
follows the old trackbed. (There are cycle
lock up and securing posts in the car
park.) From the outside it may look a little
time-worn but inside it's a fine place,
with simply furnished rooms on several
levels, two bars and a dining area,
all with great views of the surrounding
countryside. A blazing log fire in a grand
stone fireplace warms the lounge bar
in winter. Brass jugs, copper kettles
and horsebrasses hang from the beams,
while in the lounge the walls are
decorated with old golf clubs and country
paintings. There is a cellar pool room.*

Food
From a standard menu you can order fresh
cod and chips, loin of pork with apple
sauce, beef and Stilton pie, salmon and
broccoli pasta, curries, hot rolls and filled
jacket potatoes. Blackboard daily specials
favour fresh fish dishes.

Family facilities
Older children can make good use of the
pool table in the cellar. Children of all ages
are very welcome throughout the pub and
younger ones have their own standard
menu to choose from. Good summer
alfresco seating on two grassy areas,
both with country views.

Alternative refreshment stops
There are pubs at Biggin (Waterloo Inn),
Sparklow (Royal Oak); snacks at Parsley
Hay; several pubs and cafés in Hartington,
just off the route.

☞ Where to go from here
Arbor Low Henge, a major Neolithic site
near to Parsley Hay, is a significant stone
circle although the stones are now lying
flat. Small charge for entry.

Long Dale DERBYSHIRE

Along Rudyard Lake

Relive the Edwardian era on this easy route beside picturesque Rudyard Reservoir, source of the water for much of the Midlands' canal network.

Rudyard Lake

You've probably passed over, or cycled beside, many a canal and taken them for granted as part of the scenery. The building of the county's canal system was a massive undertaking, but few people consider just where the water comes from to make them operate. The answer is places like Rudyard Lake. This was created in 1800 as a reservoir to supply water to the Caldon Canal, which served Leek and, more significantly, the Trent and Mersey Canal at Stoke-on-Trent, one of Britain's most important canals.

The Dingle Brook would have taken too long to fill the reservoir (and to keep it topped up) so, in addition to the dam, a feeder channel, or leat, was constructed up in the hills to the east of Rushton Spencer.

This collects water from the River Dane as it rushes down from the high Staffordshire moors and delivers it to Rudyard.

When the North Staffordshire Railway line was built between Leek and Macclesfield during the 1840s, the owners realised the reservoir was a potential leisure resource. They ran special excursion trains and laid out walks in the area. One couple had such pleasant memories of the time they spent here they named their son Rudyard Kipling after the area. Wealthy patrons built eccentric boathouses and chalets along the western shore of the lake, and these can still be seen today.

the ride

1 This is an easy there-and-back route from **Rudyard Old Station**, now the base for the little Rudyard Lake Steam Railway. This narrow gauge line follows the course of the former standard gauge line for 1.5 miles (2.4km) along the lake shore, its miniature steam engines providing endless fascination for visitors of all ages. The route follows the track north through cool woodlands to reach the **Dam Station**. As the name suggests, this is adjacent to the dam holding back **Rudyard Lake**. Make a side detour across the dam to a **visitor centre**, café and toilets – here, too, you'll find rowing boat hire and seasonal launch trips on the lake.

Left: Boathouses at Rudyard Lake
Top: View south down Rudyard Reservoir

| 3h00 | 8.5 MILES | 13.7 KM | LEVEL 123 |

SHORTER ALTERNATIVE ROUTE

| 1h30 | 4 MILES | 6.4 KM | LEVEL 123 |

MAP: OS Explorer OL24 White Peak
START/FINISH: Rudyard Old Station, grid ref SJ955579
TRAILS/TRACKS: old railway trackbed
LANDSCAPE: wooded lake shore, peaceful pastures and meadows
PUBLIC TOILETS: Rudyard village
TOURIST INFORMATION: Leek, tel 01538 483741
CYCLE HIRE: none nearby
THE PUB: The Abbey Inn, Leek
🚴 Take care along the banks of the lake – keep well away from the shore line

Getting to the start
From Leek take the A523 north west towards Macclesfield. Soon turn left on to the B5331, signed to Rudyard Lake. The entrance to the car park is on the left immediately under the railway bridge and before Rudyard village.

Why do this cycle ride?
Rudyard Lake is surrounded by wooded hills, pleasant hay meadows and cow pastures. The route takes full advantage of the countryside and offers opportunities to enjoy the other summertime facilities here such as a miniature railway, boat trips on the lake and rowing boat hire. It's an ideal family day out.

Researched and written by: Neil Coates

2 Return to the old railway and carry on cycling northwards. The **lake** is easily visible through the trees – some care is needed as parts of the bank are prone to collapse, so keep well away from the shoreline. Looking across the lake, you'll see some of the odd boathouses that so delighted their owners a century and more ago. The lake is a popular place with school groups and Sea Scouts, so may well be lively with dinghies and Canadian canoes.

3 Passing by an intermediate railway halt, our route reaches the terminus of the miniature railway at **Hunthouse Wood**. More of the shore remains to be followed, however, so continue northwards along the old track, shortly passing through a gateway and on to a wider base of potholed, compacted ballast and cinders. The lake gradually narrows to its northern tip where there is a small **car park** and turning area. You can turn around here and retrace the route back to the start for a total ride length of 4 miles (6.4km). Before doing so it is worth diverting left along the tarred access lane for 200yds (183m) to a viewpoint offering a panorama down the length of the lake. The bridge here is across the canal feeder leat, which gathers Dingle Brook beyond the reedy marsh to the north. American troops trained for the D-Day landings in 1944 in this area, while the cornfields and pastures beyond were once a popular golf course.

Rudyard Lake

STAFFORDSHIRE

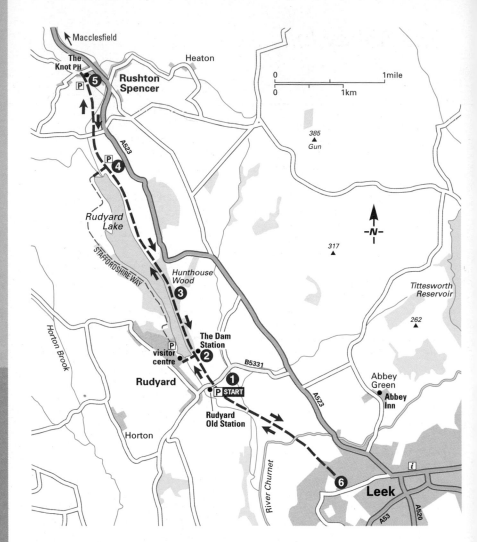

4 Back on the old railway continue to the village of **Rushton Spencer**. Look to the right of the car park for wooden bollards and the muddy railway track. Take this (not the wider potholed road) through the trees, initially a muddy stretch that soon becomes a strip of compacted gravel on a grassy trail. This leads to the old station at Rushton Spencer. There's a superb North Staffordshire Railway station house here, and also a village pub called **The Knot**.

5 This is the end of the line; from here retrace your outward route back to **Rudyard Old Station**.

6 As a final flourish it is possible to follow the old trackbed south to the outskirts of **Leek**, just short of an old tunnel. This trip is beside pastureland and partly follows the route of the canal feeder leat and the little **River Churnet**. Return the same way back to Rudyard.

The Abbey Inn

Set in beautiful countryside on the Staffordshire moorlands on the outskirts of Leek, this magnificent building enjoys an elevated position overlooking the infant Churnet Valley. It was built with stones recovered from the ruins of the nearby Cistercian Abbey of Dieu la Cresse and looks far older than its 1702 year of construction. Inside, head for the non-smoking snug bar, a super little room with bare sandstone walls, pine tables, collections of gleaming brass and copper jugs and pans, and tip-top Bass on tap. The main bar is spacious and comfortable, with a brick fireplace, photographs of old Leek town on the walls and a good mix of furnishings. From the front patio you have views along an elm-lined lane to the sandstone tower of Leek's parish church, and glimpses of the high moorlands to the north of town.

Food

From an extensive printed bar menu you can order hot filled baps, filled jacket potatoes and local favourites like steak and mushroom pudding. The limited but tempting daily specials may include sweet and sour pork, tarragon chicken in white wine sauce with mushrooms, and a good range of fish dishes.

Family facilities

The Abbey Inn has a children's licence so they are welcome anywhere in the pub and they have a standard menu to choose from. There's also a good play area (slides, climbing ropes) adjacent to the garden.

Alternative refreshment stops

The Rudyard Hotel and a café and snack bar in Rudyard village.

about the pub

The Abbey Inn
Abbey Green Road, Leek
Staffordshire ST13 8SA
Tel 01538 382865
www.abbeyinn.co.uk

DIRECTIONS: The Abbey Inn is 1.75 miles (2.8km) from Rudyard Old Station. Take the B5331 and turn right on to the A523. In 300yds (274m) turn left along Highup Road, signed for Meerbrook, and continue to a T-junction where you turn right. The Abbey Inn is 0.5 miles (800m) on the left

PARKING: 40

OPEN: all day, closed Tuesday

FOOD: daily, all day Saturday and Sunday May–September

BREWERY/COMPANY: free house

REAL ALE: Bass, guest beer

ROOMS: 2 en suite, 1 apartment

☞ Where to go from here

In Macclesfield, to the north, visit Paradise Mill and the Silk Museum which together bring to life the industry that dominated the area during the Victorian era (www.silk-macclesfield.org).

The Staffordshire Moorlands

A lovely, undulating, on-road route through the countryside where the White Peak meets the Dark Peak, visiting Longnor, that was 'Cardale' in the television series *Peak Practice*.

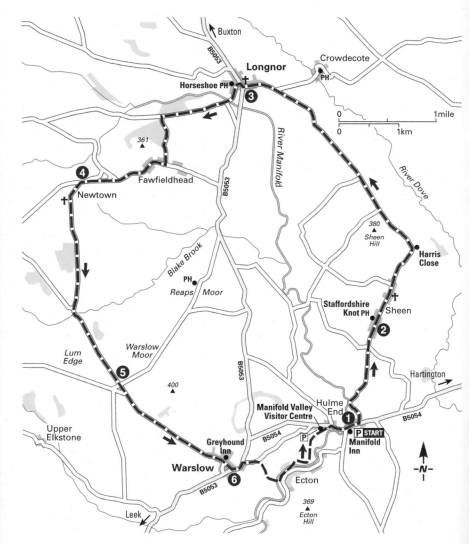

Cycling in the Manifold Valley

Manifold Valley

Before starting out, visit the Manifold Valley Visitor Centre at Hulme End. This is housed in the former village railway station and offers a fascinating glimpse into the history of the area. A series of information boards tells the story of the Manifold Valley, its remarkable geological heritage and of the light railway that once served this remote community. The canary-yellow carriages and tough little engines last ran in 1934, but a working model in the building helps evoke a sense of place. While you're there, take particular note of the board detailing the heritage to be seen at Ecton, the first station down the line from Hulme End. This is where your return route joins the trackbed of the old railway, and there is much to see including, in summer, rare plants that cling to the spoil tips of the former copper mines, once the most profitable mines in England.

While cycling across the edge of Warslow Moor keep a sharp look out for little owls. They hunt throughout the day and, true to their name, are only about 8in (21cm) high. You may spot one perched on a favourite fencepost, looking for voles or their favourite food – a large beetle.

the ride

1 Take the short steep climb up the B5054 road outside the **Manifold Inn** to a junction on the left signposted '**Sheen & Longnor**'. This winding lane initially descends before starting a gradual climb between limestone walls. Sight lines on

3h30 | **13 MILES** | **21 KM** | **LEVEL 123**

MAP: OS Explorer OL24 White Peak

START/FINISH: the Manifold Inn, grid ref SK108593

TRAILS/TRACKS: all on-road apart from a short section of the Manifold Trail at the end

LANDSCAPE: upland pastures, moorland, limestone gorge

PUBLIC TOILETS: Manifold Valley Visitor Centre, Hulme End; Longnor Market Square

TOURIST INFORMATION: Leek, tel 01538 483741

CYCLE HIRE: Parsley Hay on the High Peak Trail, 4 miles (6.4km) from Hulme End, tel 01298 84493

THE PUB: Manifold Inn, Hulme End, see Point **1** on route

🚲 Take care on the short sections of busier road at the start, just beyond Longnor, before Warslow and the very short section of B-road at Warslow. Suitable for older children with on-road cycling experience and not adverse to the odd challenging hill climb

Getting to the start

Hulme End is on the B5054 west of Hartington. Ask at the Manifold Inn if you can park and ride. Alternatively, cross the river bridge and drive to the pay car park at the Manifold Valley Visitor Centre at Hulme End, then cycle to the Manifold Inn.

Why do this cycle ride?

This route rises easily to pleasant back roads across the gritstones of the eastern fringes of the Staffordshire moorlands. The highlight of the route is the little market village of Longnor. The final section is a descent into the Manifold Valley.

Researched and written by: Neil Coates

Hulme End STAFFORDSHIRE

this section are not good, but they improve after a slightly steeper pitch brings the route to the straggling village of **Sheen**.

2 The road undulates through the village, with good views across the walled pastures to the higher Staffordshire moorlands. Passing by the village inn, the **Staffordshire Knot**, and then the little **church**, the way again steepens slightly as it rises through a few bends to level out past **Harris Close Farm**, with **Sheen Hill**'s rugged top drawing the eye left. Down to the right are occasional views into the limestone valley of the young **River Dove** and across to the knolly hills beyond. A long, easy ride follows, cresting to fall down a fairly short, sharp hill with bad sight lines. At the junction keep ahead to reach **Longnor**; from this short section are views across to the hamlet of Crowdecote and up the Dove to the sharp peaks of Chrome and Parkhouse hills.

3 At the heart of Longnor is the **Market Square**. This route crosses straight over the junction here, in front of the **Horseshoe pub** and along a lane signposted '**Royal Cottage and Leek**'. Once out of the village there's a steep descent to a bridge over the **River Manifold**, heralding the start of a long steady climb up the valley side. On the right is the imposing old village **sawmill**, being transformed into apartments. In 0.5 mile (800m) the route levels along a long tree-lined straight to reach a left turn signposted '**Fawfieldhead and Newtown**'. Follow this through to a T-junction and turn right along a pleasant undulating lane with pleasing views.

4 At a telephone box turn left along a lane signposted '**Warslow**'. Soon you'll pass by the little **chapel** at **Newtown** (built 1837) off to your right in its overgrown churchyard. This is an airy, easy cruise along a high road, with the distinctive limestone hills at Ecton the main feature off to your left beyond **Reaps Moor**. Beyond a house called Hayshead the lane starts a long, gradual climb before levelling out beside **Lum Edge** and **Warslow Moor**.

5 Go straight across the crossroads and then bear left at the junction, joining a quite well-used road that rises gradually, soon crossing a cattle grid. Cresting another rise, there's a long, sweeping descent into **Warslow**, passing the **Greyhound Inn** to reach a junction with the B5053.

6 Turn left along this road and remain on it for about 200yds (183m) to find a lane on the right, signposted 'Unsuitable for Heavy Goods Vehicles'. Carefully turn into this, which drops increasingly steeply as a narrow, winding lane. Keep right to descend to a bridge across the **Manifold**. Just beyond this turn left along the **Manifold Way** and follow this to **Hulme End**. Rejoin the main road and turn right to return to the nearby **Manifold Inn**.

A quiet lane that is perfect for cyclists near the Manifold Railway Visitor Centre

Manifold Inn

about the pub

Manifold Inn
Hulme End, Hartington
Buxton, Derbyshire SK17 0EX
Tel 01298 84537
www.themanifoldinn.co.uk

DIRECTIONS: see Getting to the start
PARKING: 25
OPEN: daily, all day Friday, Saturday and
Sunday May–September
FOOD: daily
BREWERY/COMPANY: free house
REAL ALE: Hartington, Pedigree, changing
guest beers
ROOMS: 10 en suite

Standing beside a bridge over the River Manifold and sheltered by a stand of pines, the Manifold Inn is a lovely, imposing, gabled stone building, originally built as a coaching inn some 200 years ago. Its fortunes were rejuvenated when the Leek and Manifold Light Railway opened in 1904 and it changed its name to The Light Railway Hotel, a name it retained until 1984 (50 years after the line closed). Inside, the only public room is comfortable and well presented – a solid wood bar fronts a carpeted room with plenty of beams, horse brasses, old photos and paintings of the pub, with a large wood-burning stove taking pride of place.

Food

The ever-changing chalkboard menu featuring good, home-cooked food may list home-made soups or chicken liver pâté for starters, with mains ranging from haddock, chips and mushy peas, and lasagne to lamb shank with minted *jus*, beef Wellington and grilled lemon sole. There are lighter snacks at lunchtime.

Family facilities

Children are welcome away from the bar. There is a new children's menu and smaller portions are available. The place is very popular with families. The good summer garden is shaded by mature trees.

Alternative refreshment stops

There are pubs on the route at Sheen (Staffordshire Knot), Longnor (4 pubs) and Warslow (the Greyhound Inn). Cafés and tea rooms at Longnor.

☞ Where to go from here

Blackbrook Zoological Park (at Winkhill, south west of Hulme End, off the A523) is a rare breeds centre specialising in birds, but with some mammals, reptiles, tropical fish and a children's petting corner (www.blackbrookzoologicalpark.co.uk).

Hulme End STAFFORDSHIRE

Middleton Top and the High Peak Trail

Fascinating industrial heritage and huge views on this moderate ride along an old railway designed and engineered as a canal.

High Peak Trail

The High Peak Trail is an engineering marvel. It follows the trackbed of the Cromford and High Peak Railway, built between 1825 and 1830, and was one of the world's first railways. Curiously, it was designed as a canal to link the Cromford Canal at Cromford, in the Derwent Valley, with the Upper Peak Forest tramroad and canal network in the Goyt Valley, south east of Manchester. The promoters eventually realised that water supply would be an insurmountable problem, so the route was redrafted as a railway, with the planned flights of locks replaced by steep inclines (the stations, however, retained their watery origins and were known as 'Wharfs'). One such incline tops-out at Middleton Top. Here, the engine house that provided the steam power to drive the ropes that winched the wagons up these slopes is still operational, and regular steamings are held each year. The nearby Hopton Incline was, at 1:14, the steepest gradient to be used by standard steam locomotives during the mid-20th century.

the ride

1 Take time to explore **Middleton Top** before setting out along the long straight westwards. The first feature of interest is the short **Hopton Tunnel**, a covered access to one of the many local quarries that dapple these limestone slopes around Middleton Moor. The track then passes above one of the large surviving works that still makes use of the abundant limestone – cement is a major product here.

2 After this easy start you'll soon reach the foot of the **Hopton Incline**. This is the last of the inclines used to raise the railway up from the Derwent Valley; this particular one is a steep 1:14; challenging, but an easier gradient than some of the others. Ride it or walk it, but once at the top you can take in the first of the views that characterise the High Peak Trail. At the incline top is another old incline house, while south is a ruinous windmill tower on Carsington Pasture. Secreted beyond these windy upland pastures is the valley of the Henmore Brook, now flooded as **Carsington Water**.

3 One advantage of these inclines is a very easy gradient. Once past the incline house there are several long straights and gentle curves and only a few shallow cuttings to spoil the views. Another works is passed at the foot of the stepped hillside of **Harboro Rocks**; this is renowned locally for rock climbing. A long curve

Cyclists passing an old quarry near Minninglow

exposes distant views to the north across the Peak District before the industrial hamlet of **Longcliffe** is reached. Surviving here are an engine shed and, more unusually, a watering ramp. Tankers of water would be stationed here to allow the locomotives to take on water in an area otherwise largely devoid of this vital resource. This is one opportunity to turn around – the return distance from the start is 7 miles (11.3km).

4 Continuing north west soon brings you to an incredible **viewpoint** across the north Midlands – more than 40 miles (64.3km) on a clear day. Near to hand are the unusual, craggy wooded hilltops above **Brassington; Rainster Rocks** and **Black Rocks** were home to Iron-Age families. The character of the route begins to change. Long straights on barely-raised banks of ballast or shallow cuttings give way to more extensive engineering works. A length of wood fencing to each side of the track shields you from the winds as you cross the first of a series of embankments that make the Cromford and High Peak line one of the wonders of the early railway age.

5 A little further along, a more substantial embankment is crossed. This does not have any fencing so ensure that inexperienced children are well supervised. Beyond the embankment is the rusty remnant of an old quarry crane. The most spectacular embankment comes into view as you approach **Minninglow**.

6 The picnic area beyond here is an ideal place to terminate your outward journey before returning to Middleton Top.

4h00 · **13 MILES** · **21 KM** · **LEVEL 1 2 3**

SHORTER ALTERNATIVE ROUTE

2h30 · **7 MILES** · **11.3 KM** · **LEVEL 1 2 3**

MAP: OS Explorer OL24 White Peak

START/FINISH: Middleton Top car park and visitor centre, grid ref SK275552

TRAILS/TRACKS: Old railway trackbed throughout; compacted stone or cinder surfaces

LANDSCAPE: edge of the White Peak Plateau, with dramatic views across the north Midlands

PUBLIC TOILETS: Middleton Top

TOURIST INFORMATION: Matlock Bath, tel 01629 55082

CYCLE HIRE: Middleton Top, tel 01629 823204

THE PUB: The Rising Sun, Middleton

🛈 Generally easy riding but note the 1:14 Hopton Incline and the unfenced embankment at Point 5

Getting to the start

Middleton Top car park on the High Peak Trail, just south west of Cromford, is signposted off the B5035 Ashbourne to Cromford road.

Why do this cycle ride?

There is some fascinating industrial heritage hereabouts, much of which can seen along the High Peak Trail. This route can be as long or short as you choose; the old railway climbs up inclines, strides across massive embankments and reveals superb views deep into the Midlands. Whether you're intent on an hour's ride or an afternoon's outing, this is the ideal route for a family group.

Researched and written by: Neil Coates

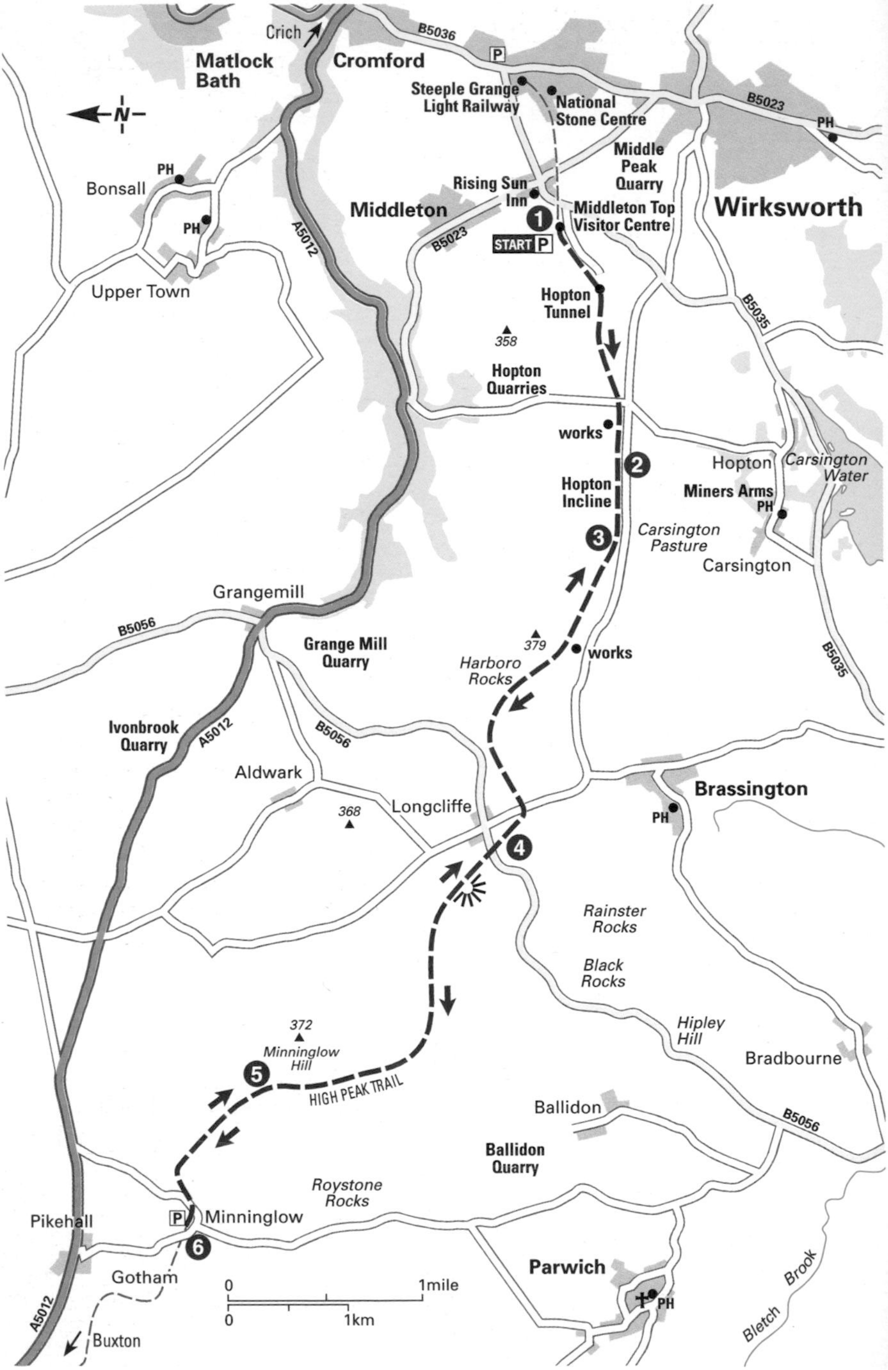

Crich

Matlock Bath

Cromford

B5036

P

Steeple Grange Light Railway

National Stone Centre

B5023

PH

Bonsall

PH

PH

Middle Peak Quarry

Rising Sun Inn

Middleton

Wirksworth

B5023

Middleton Top Visitor Centre

START P

Upper Town

A5012

①

Hopton Tunnel

358

Hopton Quarries

works

Hopton Incline

②

Hopton

Carsington Water

Miners Arms PH

③

Carsington Pasture

Carsington

Grangemill

B5056

Grange Mill Quarry

379

works

B5035

Ivonbrook Quarry

A5012

B5056

Harboro Rocks

Aldwark

Longcliffe

368

④

Brassington

PH

Rainster Rocks

Black Rocks

Hipley Hill

Bradbourne

372

Minninglow Hill

⑤

HIGH PEAK TRAIL

Ballidon

B5056

Ballidon Quarry

Pikehall

P

Minninglow

⑥

Roystone Rocks

Gotham

Parwich

PH

Buxton

Bletch Brook

0   1mile

0   1km

The Rising Sun

about the pub

The Rising Sun
Rise End
Middleton-by-Wirksworth
Derbyshire DE4 4LS
Tel 01629 822420

DIRECTIONS: load up your bikes from the Middleton Top car park and return to the main road and turn left. The Rising Sun is on the left soon after passing beneath the railway bridge

PARKING: 30

OPEN: daily, all day

FOOD: daily

BREWERY/COMPANY: Punch Taverns

REAL ALE: Tetley, Marston's Pedigree, guest beer

ROOMS: 3 bedrooms

Located on the edge of this old industrial village, the Rising Sun is an unpretentious and thriving community pub that offers a genuine welcome to all. Following your exertions on the High Peak Trails, it is a friendly place to relax in, with a lively bar and taproom plus a couple of quieter side rooms for families. The beer is good and the food home cooked. It is simply furnished throughout, with benches and traditional pub tables and chairs on quarry tiled or boarded floors, and one room features a changing gallery of paintings by a local artist.

Food

Expect traditional pub food in the form of lasagne, Brie crumble, mixed grill, plaice stuffed with prawns and mushroom sauce and fish pie. There's also a good range of sandwiches and filled potatoes.

Family facilities

Families are welcome to sit and eat in the two side rooms off the bar. There's a bargain standard children's menu and smaller portions are available. The small side garden is ideal for summer eating and drinking, or a game of boules.

Alternative refreshment stops

There is a snack bar at Middleton Top. The Miner's Arms in Brassington is about 1 mile (1.6km) off the route.

☛ Where to go from here

The National Stone Centre near Middleton is full of geological and industrial wonders explaining the structure of the Peak District, and you can take part in gem panning and fossil-rubbing. The National Tramway Museum at Crich offers vintage tram travel in period streets (www.tramway.co.uk).

The Five Pits Trail

Follow an undulating off-road route between former coal mines transformed into peaceful lakes and parks.

Former Coalfield

Sparse remnants of the Derbyshire section of the old Yorks, Notts and Derby Coalfield are now a delightful string of picnic areas, fisheries, country parks and nature reserves interlinked by the Five Pits Trail. Reclamation and conservation efforts over the past 30 years have seen spoil tips and wasteland replaced by rich hay meadows and maturing woodland, while the areas of water have attracted upwards of 200 species of birds. The former collieries had a long death, with deep mines gradually being replaced by huge opencast workings, which had a lifespan of less than 20 years.

Today's landscape holds only the barest scars of these workings, and these are slowly being disguised. The cornfields and pastures, meadows and woodland are probably the greenest this area has been for 150 years. Mining still plays its part, however. The fine bird reserves at Williamthorpe Ponds are partially filled by water pumped up from old workings from miles around. This is at a constant 10°C, and in winter attracts countless water birds to a frost- and ice-free home.

the ride

1 The **Tibshelf Ponds picnic site**, a popular place with locals and fishermen, is a picturesque mix of wooded glades, meadows and ponds where Tibshelf Colliery stood. The route is known as the Five Pits Trail, recalling busier days in this part of Derbyshire. Turn left from the car park, passing between ponds and up a short incline to a cross track. A **Five Pits Trail** board indicates the way back left, an initially rough path that soon meets a graded path, which you follow right. In a short distance you'll reach the rear of the **Wheatsheaf pub** and a descent beneath a road through an underpass. Rising again, turn right on to the compacted track. Crossing a rough lane, the way drops steeply down; don't speed, as the surface is badly rutted. This descent is matched by a long gradual climb and, soon, **Hardstoft Lane** picnic site.

2 Cross the road here, continuing along the firm track to reach **Locko Plantation**, planted in 1970, a mix of spruce, sweet chestnut and other strong growing species that clothe the remnants of the old spoil heaps at Pilsley Colliery. A very steep descent ends at a gate; carefully cross and pick up the trail opposite, rising again to cross **Timber Lane** into another picnic area. The track leaves left from the rear of this, rising gently to a junction. Here keep left, heading for **Grassmoor**. The next road crossing at the edge of **Williamthorpe** is rather busier, so take care here.

3 The next junction is at **Wolfie Pond**. Here, keep left for **Grassmoor** before forking right just before a gate. The open meadows here are typical of the reclaimed areas; more await you at **Grassmoor Country Park**, the end of the line. Spend time exploring the thickets, hay meadows and ponds before returning to an overbridge to commence the return journey.

4 A long, gradual climb returns you to **Wolfie Pond**, where you turn left for **Williamthorpe**. After a while pass through the outskirts of an industrial estate built on the site of another old colliery. A steep descent brings you to a wide bridge across a brook. Turn right along the wheelchair route, passing the large ponds before, at the far end, turning sharp left up an incline for **Holmewood**. Pause at the crossways at the top and look left to spot the distant, crooked spire of Chesterfield's parish church. Your way is right, soon reaching **Holmewood Bridge**. Dismount here, cross the bridge and rejoin the **Five Pits Trail** on the left, shortly crossing a busy road.

5 Pleasant woodland is superceded by cornfields and meadows before the outward route is rejoined at a junction. Follow signs for **Tibshelf** from here, crossing lanes with care.

6 Excellent views to the right (west) encompass the distant edge of the Peak District and the war memorial above **Crich**. Beyond the Wheatsheaf underpass, follow the trail back to **Tibshelf Ponds**, turning left at the lane to the car park.

Along the Five Pits Trail near Tibshelf

3h30 — **11.5 MILES** — **18.4 KM** — **LEVEL 1 2 3**

MAP: OS Explorer 269 Chesterfield & Alfreton

START/FINISH: Tibshelf Ponds picnic area, grid ref SK441600

TRAILS/TRACKS: old railway and hard-surfaced tracks

LANDSCAPE: mixed immature woodland, hay meadows and cornfields, with views across Derbyshire to the Peak District

PUBLIC TOILETS: none on route

TOURIST INFORMATION: Chesterfield, tel 01246 345777

CYCLE HIRE: none near by

THE PUB: Weeping Ash Country Inn, Hardstoft

❶ Care to be taken at the road crossings. There are some short, steep climbs and some longer, gentler inclines

Getting to the start

From Chesterfield head south on the A61 through Clay Cross, turning on to the B6014 eastbound at Stretton (signed Tibshelf). At the edge of Tibshelf turn right on to the B6025, then very shortly left on the B6026 for Newton. In 300yds (274m) turn left into Shetland Road. In 500yds (457m) turn right into Sunny Bank. The car park is at the end of this road.

Why do this cycle ride?

This is a lovely ride along old railways and colliery tracks, long since reclaimed and now a green corridor between the resurgent pit villages of this part of Derbyshire. Excellent countryside and a fascinating heritage offer a moderately challenging route within sight of the edge of the Peak District.

Researched and written by: Neil Coates

Five Pits Trail **DERBYSHIRE**

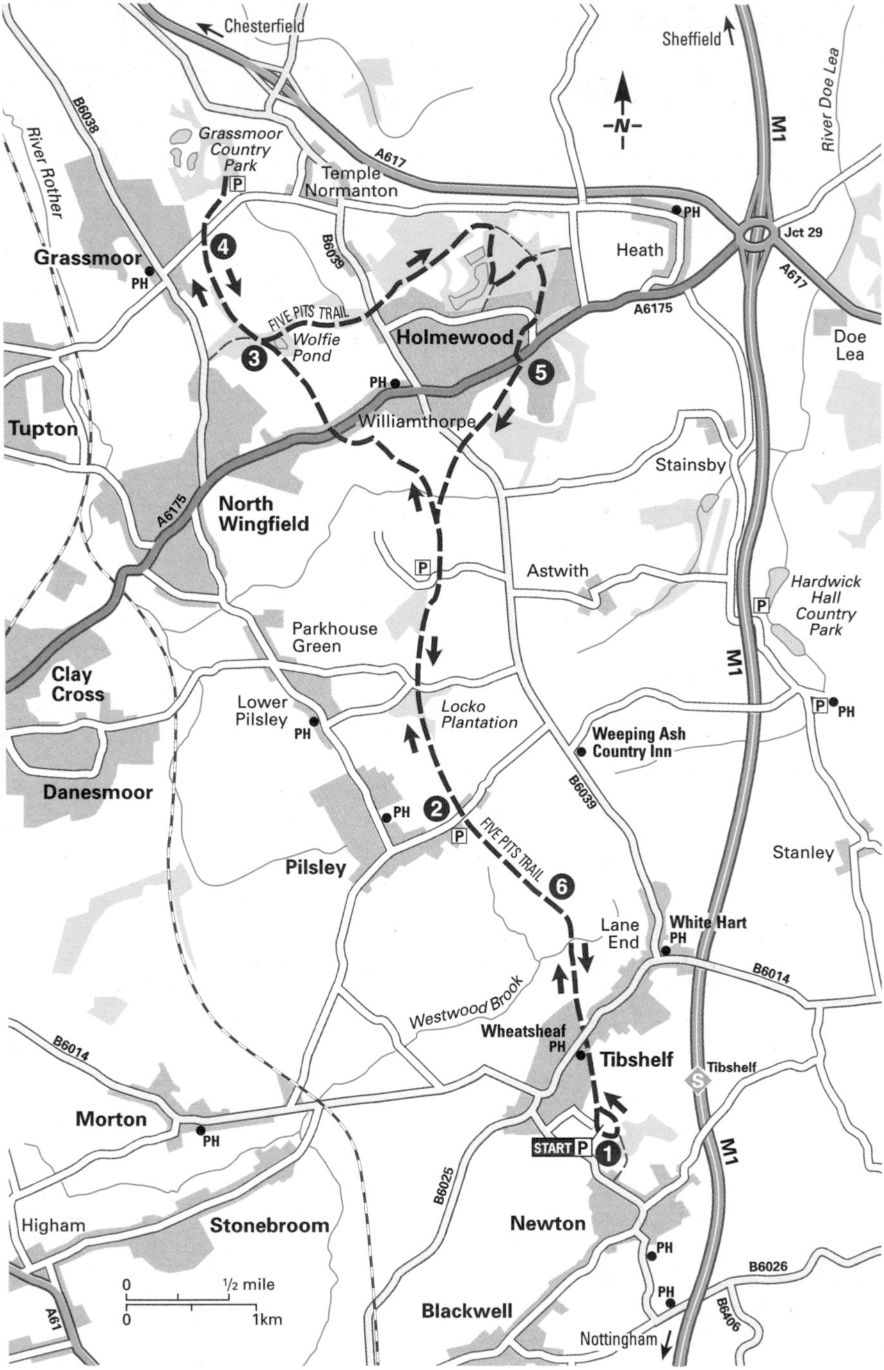

Five Pits Trail DERBYSHIRE

Chesterfield

Sheffield

M1

River Doe Lea

B6038

River Rother

Grassmoor
Country
Park
P

Temple
Normanton

A617

PH

Jct 29

A617

Heath

4

Grassmoor

PH

B6039

Holmewood

A6175

Doe
Lea

3

FIVE PITS TRAIL
Wolfie
Pond

5

Tupton

PH

Williamthorpe

Stainsby

A6175

North
Wingfield

P

Astwith

Hardwick
Hall
Country
Park

P

M1

Clay
Cross

Parkhouse
Green

Locko
Plantation

P

PH

Danesmoor

Lower
Pilsley

PH

2

Weeping Ash
Country Inn

B6039

Stanley

Pilsley

PH

P

FIVE PITS TRAIL

6

Lane
End

White Hart
PH

B6014

Westwood Brook

Wheatsheaf
PH

Tibshelf

Tibshelf

S

B6014

Morton

PH

START P

1

Newton

M1

PH

B6025

Higham

Stonebroom

PH

A61

Blackwell

Nottingham

B6026

B6406

-N-

0   1/2 mile
0   1km

Weeping Ash Country Inn

about the pub

Weeping Ash Country Inn
Hardstoft, Chesterfield
Derbyshire S45 8AE
Tel 01246 850276

DIRECTIONS: from the Tibshelf Ponds
car park return to the B6026 and the mini-
roundabout accessing Tibshelf High Street.
Turn right up the High Street and go through
the village to a mini-roundabout at the White
Hart pub. Turn left for Chesterfield (B6039)
and drive for a mile (1.6km); the pub is on
the right at a junction

PARKING: 50

OPEN: daily, eves only Monday to Friday

FOOD: no food Sunday evening

BREWERY/COMPANY: free house

REAL ALE: Farmers, seasonal beers

ROOMS: 7 bedrooms

---

*The Weeping Ash is a very comfortable
and well-appointed country inn, catering
for loyal local drinkers, a good passing
trade and guests using the inn as a
base for exploring this peaceful part
of Derbyshire. As you would expect,
weeping ash trees surround this
rambling stone-built inn which stands in
the heart of Hardstoft. Country sporting
paraphernalia (gin traps, fishing rods,
gun cases), local photographs, and a
collection of porcelain adorn the walls
and window sills within the comfortably
furnished interior, which comprises a
'locals' bar, two lounge bars and two*
*neatly laid-up dining areas. You'll find
winter log fires, decent ale and a genuine
warm welcome for walkers and cyclists.
Bedrooms are housed in tastefully
converted outbuildings.*

Food

From a wide ranging bar menu, opt for
the traditional chilli, liver and onions,
bangers and mash or hot filled rolls or look
to the specials board for something more
imaginative, perhaps loin of venison with
red wine and rosemary *jus* or pork loin
on buttered mash with smoked bacon
and cream sauce. There is a separate
restaurant menu.

Family facilities

Children can let off steam in the play area
by the car park and on fine days families
can make good use of the small patio
areas. Children are very welcome indoors
where younger family members have their
own menu.

Alternative refreshment stops

There are plenty of pubs and shops
in Tibshelf.

☛ Where to go from here

Hardwick Hall, one of the most magnificent
Elizabethan mansions in England, houses
remarkable tapestries, furniture and
woodwork (www.nationaltrust.org.uk).

Along the Manifold

Follow England's oldest multi-user trail on an easy ride through woodland, deep gorges and past spectacular caves above part-time rivers.

Disappearing rivers

If you are enjoying this ride in the summer months, then mention of rivers may strike you as a mistake. There's no water to be seen in the first 4.5 miles (7.2km) of the route, and only intermittently thereafter. The reason is that the underlying rock is limestone and as this is extremely porous the water cannot, except in the wettest weather, maintain a flow at the surface. Instead, it trickles away down 'swallets' to carve a remarkable underground course through fissures, passages and caves which are not necessarily directly beneath the dry riverbeds.

Both the River Hamps and the Manifold exhibit this characteristic. Their combined waters eventually resurface in the National Trust's estate at Ilam, a few miles towards Ashbourne. In place of the water are rivers of green. These are the enormous leaves of butterbur, which thrive in damp places and can survive the occasional flood of water after a particularly heavy downpour. It's at Dafar Bridge, just before you reach Wettonmill, that the waters are seen permanently at the surface. At the series of swallets here, an eccentric Edwardian spent a fortune burying iron pipes into the river bed in an attempt to create real 'Water Music' by means of differing pressures as the water disappeared underground. Success was elusive!

the ride

1 The signal box at the old station is the starting point. The station itself was an interchange between the standard gauge line to Leek and the narrow gauge Leek and Manifold Light Railway. This 2ft 6in gauge line meandered through these remote valleys between 1904 and 1934, and this is the route we now follow. The ride soon joins a wide cycle-pavement beside the main road. On reaching the crossing point, carefully cross into the 'No Traffic' lane opposite. You'll immediately cross a bridge over the **River Hamps**, one of many such crossings in the next few miles. It's an easy trip along the tarred way, curving this way and that towards the enclosing valley sides.

2 Soon after **Lee House Farm** is passed (teas and meals here in season) the ash woods close in and the route becomes tunnel-like beneath these bird-rich boughs. In 2 miles (3.2km) the route curves gradually left to reveal **Beeston Tor**. In the caravan field on your right here, note the old green hut, the former refreshment room of Beeston Tor Station. Here, also, the Hamps meets with the River Manifold, flowing south beneath the Tor towards the distant River Dove. The route now runs parallel to an access road before reaching a gateway and a lane at **Weag's Bridge**.

3 Carefully cross straight over and ride through the car park to and through the gate at the end, regaining a non-trafficked

The imposing site of Thor's Cave

MAP: OS Explorer OL24 White Peak

START/FINISH: Waterhouses Old Station, grid ref SK085503

TRAILS/TRACKS: the entire route is tarred, some of it badly pitted, about 3 miles (4.8km) is shared with light road traffic, one tunnel

LANDSCAPE: limestone gorges, ash woods and good views towards the moorlands

PUBLIC TOILETS: Waterhouses and Hulme End stations.

TOURIST INFORMATION: Leek, tel 01538 483741

CYCLE HIRE: Waterhouses Old Station, tel 01538 308609; also Brown End Farm, tel 01538 308313

THE PUB: Ye Olde Crown Hotel, Waterhouses, near Point **1** on route

stretch. This is probably the most spectacular part of the valley, the river gyrating between immensely steep cliffs cloaked in some of England's finest ash woods. As the route leaves the trees around a left-hand curve, stop to look back to see the awesome location of **Thor's Cave**, high above the valley. An interpretation board tells its history; a steep path leads up to it.

4 The tortuous road between Wetton and Grindon is soon reached at a gated bridge. Beyond here, and for the next 3 miles (4.8km), you will share the road with other traffic, so care is needed. It's easier to continue ahead along the flatter route marking the old railway (the other road here loops back in after 0.5 miles/800m) to reach the popular tea rooms at **Wetton Mill**. Beware of traffic here at another minor junction. This is a good place to turn around if you are taking the shorter alternative route (9 miles/14.5km round trip).

5 Continuing north, the road keeps company with the river to reach **Swainsley Tunnel**. This is shared with vehicles, but is wide enough for bike and car and also well lit. At the far end go ahead back on to a segregated track, cycling north to pass beneath bald **Ecton Hill** and its sombre mining remains. Crossing another road here, the valley sides gradually pull back for the final approach to journey's end, the station at **Hulme End**.

6 Turn around here and retrace your route back to the start. Take care at **Weag's Bridge** to take the gated lane rather than the access road to the caravan site at Beeston Tor Farm.

Getting to the start

Waterhouses Old Station is in the village of Waterhouses, on the A523 about half-way between Leek and Ashbourne. Turn up the road beside Ye Olde Crown Hotel, pass beneath the railway overbridge and turn left into the car park, continuing to the cycle hire centre at the top end.

Why do this cycle ride?

The scenery of the Hamps and Manifold valleys should be enough to tempt anyone on to this trail which follows the trackbed of a former narrow gauge railway through lime-stone gorges, and passing by the tantalising remains of the old railway and the industries it served. The terminus at Hulme End has an excellent Visitor and Interpretative Centre.

Researched and written by: Neil Coates

Manifold STAFFORDSHIRE

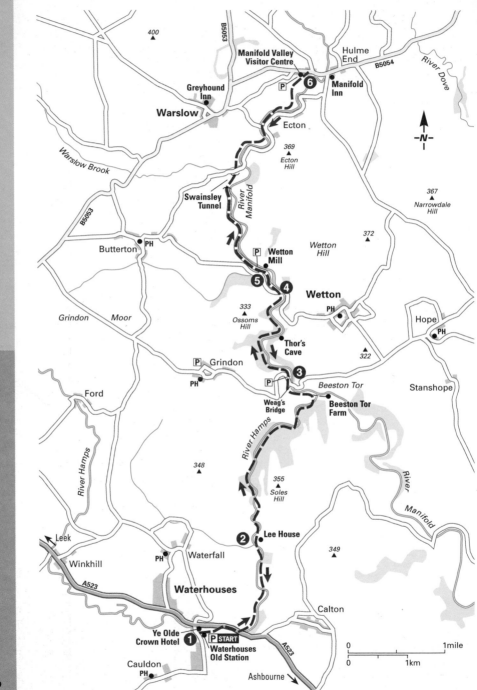

400

B5053

Manifold Valley
Visitor Centre

Hulme
End

B5054

River Dove

Greyhound
Inn

P

6

Manifold
Inn

Warslow

Ecton

Warslow Brook

369
▲
Ecton
Hill

367
▲
Narrowdale
Hill

**Swainsley
Tunnel**

River
Manifold

B5053

372
▲

Wetton
Hill

PH

Butterton

P

**Wetton
Mill**

5

4

Wetton

PH

Hope

PH

Grindon   Moor

333
▲
Ossoms
Hill

P   Grindon

PH

**Thor's
Cave**

322
▲

Stanshope

Ford

P

3

Beeston Tor

Weag's
Bridge

**Beeston Tor
Farm**

River
Manifold

River Hamps

River Hamps

348
▲

355
▲
Soles
Hill

Leek

2

Lee House

349
▲

PH

Waterfall

Winkhill

A523

Waterhouses

Calton

**Ye Olde
Crown Hotel**

1

P START

**Waterhouses
Old Station**

A523

Cauldon

PH

Ashbourne

–N–

0 _____ 1mile

0 _____ 1km

50

Ye Olde Crown Hotel

about the pub

Ye Olde Crown Hotel
Waterhouses, Stoke-on-Trent
Staffordshire ST10 3HL
Tel 01538 308204

DIRECTIONS: see Getting to the start
PARKING: 20
OPEN: daily
FOOD: daily
BREWERY/COMPANY: Banks Brewery
REAL ALE: Marston's, Burton Bitter
ROOMS: 4 bed B&B cottage

A traditional village local on the banks of the River Hamps, Ye Olde Crown dates from around 1648 when it was built as a coaching inn. Inside are two bars, each sporting original stonework and solid beams, the latter adorned with old water jugs. Log fires are lit in cooler weather. The lounge bar with its Edwardian darkwood half-panelled walls, wall benches and a vast array of copper and brass pieces, provides a comfortable retreat for a traditional pub meal and a pint of Tetleys after a good walk. Homely accommodation includes an adjacent cottage.

Food

Offering a traditional range of pub food, dishes are freshly prepared and take in fish and chips, home-made pies, ham, lasagne, jacket potatoes, sandwiches and filled baguettes. The weekly roast is served until 6pm on Sundays.

Family facilities

Families will find a friendly welcome towards children who have their own good-value menu to choose from. Unfortunately, summer al fresco seating and eating is limited to a few tables by the car park.

Alternative refreshment stops

There are tea rooms at Lee House Farm and Wetton Mill along the route. The Yew Tree pub at Cauldon, just 1 mile (1.6km) from the cycle hire centre and along the same road, has a remarkable collection of polyphons, automatic pianos and curlos, a great favourite with children.

☛ Where to go from here

The Churnet Valley Railway, based at Cheddleton near Leek, operates steam trains into the beautiful Churnet Valley (www.churnet-valley-railway.co.uk).

Thor's Cave in the Manifold Valley

Tissington Trail · DERBYSHIRE

Along the Tissington Trail

An easy ride from the Tissington estate village along an old railway line above the secluded valley of the Bletch Brook.

Dew Ponds

Once beyond the old station at Alsop, one feature of the landscape you'll notice along the route are the occasional small ponds in the pastures – these are dew ponds. The name comes from the belief that morning dew would provide sufficient water for cattle and sheep to drink. In days gone by these would be hollows dug out and lined with clay to stop the water from draining away. As this is an area where the rock is predominantly porous limestone, rainwater seeps away and surface water is very rare. The modern-day versions are watertight and they don't rely on dew, either, as they are regularly topped up by the farmers.

Summertime on the Tissington Trail sees a profusion of butterflies, with the Common Blue one of the most noticeable. This very small insect feeds largely on clover flowers and the bright yellow flowers of bird's foot trefoil, a low-growing plant that flourishes in limestone areas. Another butterfly to look out for is the colourful Red Admiral which lays its eggs on nettles, the food plant of the caterpillar.

the ride

1 The Tissington car park is at the site of the old railway station. Take time to find the information board which has a fine picture of the place in its heyday. There's also a village information board here; the village centre is only a short cycle away and it's well worth taking the loop before starting out. Turn left from the car park entrance, then right along **Chapel Lane**. This passes one of the five wells that are dressed with flowers during the famous Well Dressing Ceremony held in in the village in May on Ascension Day. The lane rises gently to a junction at the top of the village. Turn left to drop down the main street, lined by greens and passing **Tissington Hall** and more wells. At the bottom keep left, passing the village pond before swinging right to return to the car park. Here turn left, passing beneath a bridge to join the old trackbed, which starts a long, easy climb.

2 This initial stretch is through a wooded cutting, soon shallowing to offer the occasional view through the trees across the glorious countryside here at the southern end of the National Park. The panorama sweeps across the peaceful valley of the **Bletch Brook** to take in the high ridge of rough pastures above **Ballidon** to the right.

3 The first natural place to turn around to return to Tissington is the car park and picnic area at the **former Alsop Station**. This would make a round trip of 6 miles (9.7km) and take perhaps 1.5 hours – and it's downhill virtually all the way back!

3h30 — **16 MILES** — **25.7 KM** — **LEVEL 1**23

SHORTER ALTERNATIVE ROUTE

1h30 — **6 MILES** — **9.7 KM** — **LEVEL 1**23

MAP: OS Explorer OL24 White Peak

START/FINISH POINT: Tissington Old Station, grid ref SK177520

TRAILS/TRACKS: old railway trackbed, lanes in Tissington village

LANDSCAPE: limestone plateau of the White Peak, extensive views

PUBLIC TOILETS: Tissington and Hartington old stations

TOURIST INFORMATION: Ashbourne, tel 01335 343666

CYCLE HIRE: Peak Cycle Hire, Mapleton Lane, Ashbourne, Derbyshire, tel 01335 343156, www.peakdistrict.org

THE PUB: Bluebell Inn, Tissington

Getting to the start

Tissington is signposted off the A515 Ashbourne to Buxton road, a few miles north of Ashbourne. Pass the pond in the village and bear right to find the gated entrance to the Tissington Trail car park.

Why do this cycle ride?

This is one of England's most famous cycling trails and, as it is an old railway line, you can simply choose just when and where to turn round and return to the start. We've suggested heading north, but you could as easily head south to the pleasant market town of Ashbourne, with its antique shops and bookshops. Going north offers a short option along a wooded route followed by a contrasting, airy route through cuttings and along embankments. It's your choice!

Researched and written by: Neil Coates

Tissington Trail

DERBYSHIRE

4 It's well worth continuing north, however, as once the old railway passes beneath the main road, the character of the Trail changes, and a more open terrain offers different views and experiences. The track continues its gentle climb, soon crossing the first of many embankments. There are grand views left (west) across the rolling pastureland of the **White Peak** towards the higher, darker hills that characterise the Staffordshire moorlands, forming the western horizon. Closer to hand are round-topped hills capped by crowns of trees.

5 Off to your left, the village of **Biggin-by-Hartington** soon appears – notice the old **army huts** down to the left, still put to good use as storerooms. In the distance and looking north, you may pick out the distinctive knolls of limestone near Longnor, Chrome Hill and Parkhouse Hill. The strand of cuttings and embankments continues towards the next logical turning point, **Hartington Old Station**. Here, the former signal box has been preserved; climb the steps to view the old points and levers.

6 This is the ideal place to turn round and retrace the route back to the car park at **Tissington**.

Top: The valley of Bletch Brook

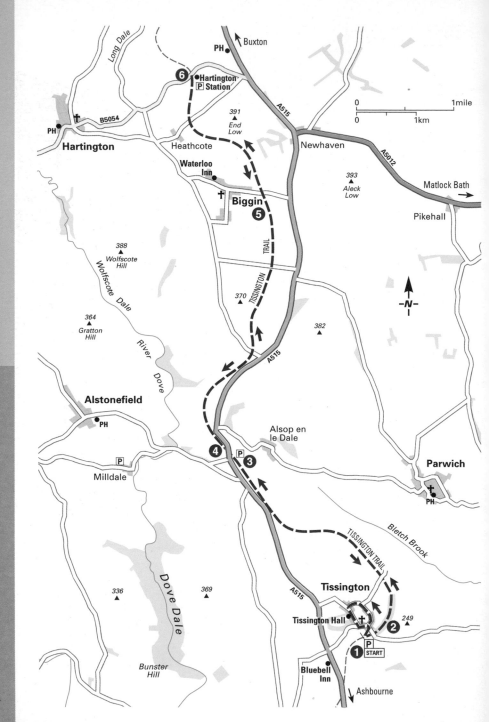

Long Dale

PH ↑ Buxton

⑥ Hartington
Ⓟ Station

391
▲
End
Low

A515

B5054 †

PH ●

Hartington

Heathcote

Newhaven

A5012

↑ Matlock Bath →

**Waterloo
Inn** ●

393
▲
Aleck
Low

Pikehall

†

Biggin

⑤

388
▲
Wolfscote
Hill

Wolfscote Dale

TRAIL

370
▲

382
▲

TISSINGTON

364
▲
Gratton
Hill

River Dove

A515

-N-

Alstonefield

PH ●

Alsop en
le Dale

Parwich

④

Ⓟ ③

†

PH

Ⓟ

Milldale

0 _____ 1mile
0 _____ 1km

Bletch Brook

TISSINGTON TRAIL

336
▲

369
▲

A515

Tissington

Dove Dale

249
▲

Tissington Hall †

②

**Bunster
Hill**

Ⓟ
① START

**Bluebell
Inn**

↓ Ashbourne

Bluebell Inn

A favourite watering hole for walkers and cyclists following a day on the Tissington Trail, the stone-built Bluebell Inn dates from 1777. In the long, beamed bar you can rest weary legs and savour a reviving pint of Hardys & Hansons bitter. Fires at either end add welcome winter warmth, while in summer vases of flowers on each table add a splash of colour to the narrow room. Prints of local scenes, framed advertisements and old photographs of the pub adorn the walls and high shelves are lined with traditional pub memorabilia. There is a light and airy dining room.

Food

The bar menu is very extensive and lists traditional pub fare. Tuck into wild mushroom lasagne, beef in ale pie, Hartington chicken, or a decent round of sandwiches. Limited daily specials may take in beef and tomato casserole, a giant Yorkshire pudding filled with scrumpy pork casserole, and local trout.

Family facilities

Familes are welcome at any time throughout the pub. There's a standard selection of children's meals, in addition to portions of lasagne and Yorkshire pudding filled with beef stew. Unfortunately the large garden is next to the busy road so keep an eye on children.

Alternative refreshment stops

There are two village tea rooms in Tissington, the Old Coach House and Bassett Wood Farm.

about the pub

Bluebell Inn
Tissington, Ashbourne
Derbyshire DE6 1NH
Tel 01335 350317
www.bluebelltissington.co.uk

DIRECTIONS: from the Tissington Trail car park turn left back through the village to the A515 and turn right to locate the pub beside the main road

PARKING: 75

OPEN: daily, all day March–November

FOOD: daily, all day March–November

BREWERY/COMPANY: Greene King Brewery

REAL ALE: 3 guest beers

☛ Where to go from here

Ilam Country Park is a National Trust estate just west of Tissington. Ten miles (16.1km) south of Ashbourne is Sudbury Hall, home to the National Trust's Museum of Childhood (www.nationaltrust.org.uk).

Around Carsington Water

Discover picturesque hamlets and abundant wildlife at one of England's largest reservoirs.

The Reservoir

Carsington Water, at the heart of the route, was opened in 1992 and is one of the largest reservoirs in England. The visitor centre tells the story of the reservoir and

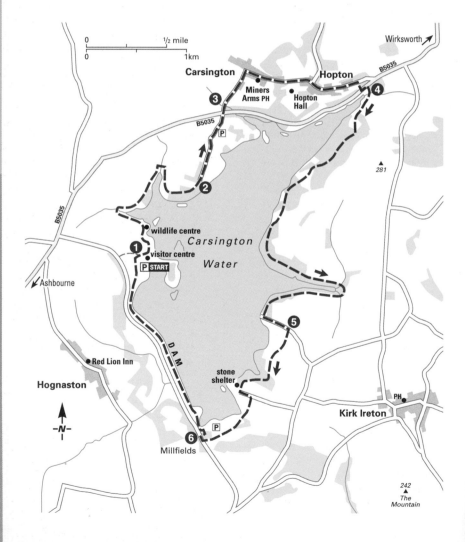

Left: Carving beside the trail around Carsington Water

the surrounding area in a display aimed largely at children who visit on school trips. The reservoir covers an area of 741 acres (300ha) and is just over 100ft (30m) at its deepest. Its location, high up above major river catchments and close to limestone uplands (although the site itself is on impermeable sandstones and shales), means that most of its water is pumped up from the River Derwent at Ambergate, which is over 6 miles (9.7km) away and is 430ft (131m) lower than the average water level in the reservoir.

It is part of a complex, interlinked series of reservoirs and aqueducts that include the massive series of lakes in the upper Derwent Valley to the west of Sheffield, supplying water to domestic and industrial consumers in places as far apart as Derby, Nottingham and Leicester. There are rowing boats for hire and, a short walk from the visitor centre, there is a Wildlife Centre with a well-equipped bird hide and displays explaining the conservation measures adopted here.

the ride

1 From the car park at the **visitor centre** look for the fingerposts pointing the way to the **wildlife centre**; this will bring you to the start of a sandy, compacted track just below the coach park. These initial stages are an easy settling in section, with a few short hills and descents, largely between hedges and offering occasional glimpses of

3h30 — **8 MILES** — **12.9 KM** — **LEVEL 123**

MAP: OS Explorer OL24 White Peak

START/FINISH: Carsington Reservoir Visitor Centre, grid ref SK241515

TRAILS/TRACKS: largely compacted gravel, sand and earth tracks, with some back lanes

LANDSCAPE: woodland and waterside

PUBLIC TOILETS: at the start and the Millfields parking area at Point 6 of the route

TOURIST INFORMATION: Ashbourne, tel 01335 343666

CYCLE HIRE: The Watersports Centre, Carsington Water, tel 01629 540478

THE PUB: Red Lion Inn, Main Street, Hognaston

🛈 Some short, steep climbs and a couple of longer ascents through woodland

Getting to the start

Carsington Water is signed from the B5035 between Ashbourne and Wirksworth. The route starts at the visitor centre on the western shore of the reservoir.

Why do this cycle ride?

This is an enjoyable circuit with a mix of level tracks, a section of road cycling on back lanes through the picturesque hamlets of Carsington and Hopton, and with more challenging ascents and descents on the eastern side of the reservoir.

Researched and written by: Neil Coates

Carsington Water

DERBYSHIRE

the reservoir. The track is partly shared with walkers and partly designated as a horse and cycle route, so be prepared to stop and obey any instruction signs.

2 The track joins a tarred farm access road, shortly passing by the **Sheepwash** car park. Take extra care here as you join the car park access road before arriving at the main road. The way is diagonally across to the left and along the minor road for Carsington.

3 There's a steady climb before the lane descends into **Carsington**, a picturesque village of old limestone cottages and houses. The local inn, the **Miners Arms**, recalls that the area was once a thriving mining community – lead ore was the staple raw material extracted hereabouts. The lane undulates gently through the village and the neighbouring hamlet of Hopton. Pass beside the remarkable wall surrounding the **Hopton Hall Estate**, a wavy barrier of bricks with square towers and rounded bays. At the far end of Hopton, pass by **Henmore Grange** before looking right for the waymarked, fenced path that drops steeply down to a gate on to the B5035.

4 Cross carefully here, go left signed for **Millfields**, and turn right along the track beyond a further safety gate. You're at the

The Visitor Centre at Carsington Water

extremity of the reservoir here, with views down the length of the lake. The first of a long series of hills is soon encountered, leading to a gate into woodlands with a wealth of wild flowers, and many short descents and longer inclines. You rise high above the waterline here before cresting a final summit to reveal views towards the dam and valve tower, and a steep hill down, passing by a wooden carving, just one of the sculptures dotted around the reservoir. When you eventually reach a short section of tarred farm lane, turn up along this to a waymarked gate, right, back on to the track.

5 Further ups and downs bring you past a **stone shelter**; take a peek inside to find some inventive wooden carvings. Just past here turn up the old lane. Pass by the farmhouse before looking right for the waymarked gateway back on to the cycle track. From here you're once again on a dedicated cycle/horse track that brings you to a gateway on to a wide grass verge by the main road. Turn right down the verge and right again into **Millfields**.

6 The waymarking is confusing here. Take the marked cycle path past the entry barriers and then go sharp left along a track. Go round a bend and along a short straight section, then dogleg left then right along a sandy track to reach the dam. At the far end head back to the **visitor centre**.

Red Lion Inn

Standing next to the squat medieval parish church, the 17th-century Red Lion is a charming traditional village inn. Expect a mix of floorboards and quarry tile flooring, a huge old stone fireplace, a carved and panelled wood bar, some exposed stone walls, and antique furnishings amidst time-worn old pub and farmhouse tables and chairs in the cosy, L-shaped main bar. In the upper bar room you'll find worn settles, old chapel chairs still with their prayer-book racks, a grandfather clock and another blazing log fire. Here you'll find bric-a-brac, country prints and old photos, while to the rear the conservatory restaurant (same menus) is altogether lighter and more modern, with colourful prints, potted plants and more contemporary furniture. There is a welcoming atmosphere throughout.

Food

From an imaginative chalkboard menu, order a starter of home-made soup with warm bread and follow with rib-eye steak from Derbyshire cattle, or tuck into roast leg of lamb with redcurrant gravy and apricot and hazelnut stuffing, or one of the daily fresh fish options, such as swordfish.

Family facilities

Children are welcome inside the bar if they are eating and smaller portions of the main menu are available. There is summer seating to the front of the pub.

Alternative refreshment stops

The Miner's Arms at Carsington; a restaurant and café at the reservoir visitor centre.

about the pub

Red Lion Inn
Main Street, Hognaston
Ashbourne, Derbyshire DE6 1PR
Tel 01335 370396
www.lionrouge.com

DIRECTIONS: The Red Lion in Hognaston, is about 1.5 miles (2.4km) from the visitor centre. Load the bikes on to the car, then turn right at the car park entrance to reach a T-junction with the B5035. Turn left, then left again signposted 'Hognaston Only'. The pub is on the left next to the church

PARKING: 25

OPEN: daily

FOOD: daily

BREWERY/COMPANY: free house

REAL ALE: Marston's Pedigree, Burton, guest beers

ROOMS: 3 double en suite

☛ Where to go from here

Ten miles (16.1km) east of Carsington is Heage Windmill (grid ref 367507) a squat stone tower built of local sandstone, with six sails (www.heagewindmill.co.uk).

The charm of the Churnet

Alton Castle, a Victorian building on the site of a Norman castle

Trace the route of an old canal and railway to the fascinating industrial village of Oakamoor.

Churnet Valley

Here and there along the way are the scant remains of the former Uttoxeter branch of the Caldon Canal. This 13-mile (20.9km) stretch was built during the early 19th century, running from the canal terminus at the vast limestone works at Froghall through to the market town of Uttoxeter, thereby connecting the town to the main canal network at Stoke-on-Trent. It lasted just 34 years before the North Staffordshire Railway bought out the canal company and built its new line along the Churnet Valley, filling in much of the canal to use as a trackbed.

One impetus for both the canal and railway was the industrial complex at

Oakamoor. It had been the site of an iron-processing centre for centuries before the industry really found its feet in the 19th century when Thomas Patten & Co developed tinplating and later copper wire foundries here. The copper came from the Duke of Sutherland's mines at Ecton, in the Manifold Valley, and was brought the short distance across the moors by packhorses. Most famously, the copper wire used in the first transatlantic telegraph cable was drawn out here before being laid across the ocean from Isambard Kingdom Brunel's *Great Eastern* steamship.

the ride

1 The route follows the trackbed of the former Churnet Valley Railway which closed in 1965. It starts at a gateway just beyond the village petrol station. Join the old line here, immediately passing between the old platforms. Once past these, the way becomes a grassy trail, with just a narrow strip of compacted gravel offering a surfaced route through the greensward. This is true of the route for the first couple of miles as it forges a way remote from any road or building. At one point it crosses the **River Churnet** and comes close to a muddy, overgrown cut, the first sign of the old canal that the railway replaced in the 1840s. The narrow track widens here and there, eventually becoming more graded as it approaches the village of **Alton**.

2 Keep an eye out for imposing **Alton Castle**. This is Victorian, built on the site of an original Norman castle by the 16th Earl of Shrewsbury and mimics some of the grandiose castles that top crags and hilltops along the Rhine gorge in central Europe. This route doesn't touch the village itself, but sweeps past the stunning old **North Staffordshire Railway (NSR) station**, now a private dwelling.

3 Passing beneath an overbridge, the trackbed runs below sandstone cliffs and beside further marshy stretches of the old canal. The gorge-like quality of the Churnet Valley is best appreciated here before the old line reaches the site of the former station at **Oakamoor**. Keep left of the old platforms here to join an access road that brings the route to the outskirts of the village at the old tunnel keeper's cottage, another striking NSR building. Turn right for the short distance to the village **car park**. It's worth securing your cycles here and following the heritage trail around this fascinating settlement with its surprising history.

4 From the car park here turn left along the lane which, beyond a left fork to join **Red Road**, rises gradually high above the river, then offers an easy passage along this quiet by-road to reach the **Rambler's Retreat** tea rooms and restaurant, a very popular stop for cyclists and walkers

2h30 — **8.5 MILES** **13.7 KM** — **LEVEL 123**

MAP: OS Explorer 259 Derby
START/FINISH: Denstone, grid ref SK100410
TRAILS/TRACKS: old railway and back lanes
LANDSCAPE: wooded river valley and old villages
PUBLIC TOILETS: none on route
TOURIST INFORMATION: Ashbourne, tel 01335 343666
CYCLE HIRE: none near by
THE PUB: The Bull's Head, High Street, Alton

Getting to the start
Denstone is on the B5032 about half-way between Cheadle and Ashbourne. In the village follow the signs for Denstone College and park at the village hall or on the roadside nearby.

Why do this cycle ride?
The Churnet Valley, one of the most peaceful and unspoilt valleys in the Midlands, is dotted with a few small villages but is otherwise remote and picturesque. This easy ride links three of these villages and takes in beautiful wooded sections along the way, encountering surprising industrial heritage and scenery reminiscent of the Rhine Valley in Germany.

Researched and written by: Neil Coates

Churnet Valley STAFFORDSHIRE

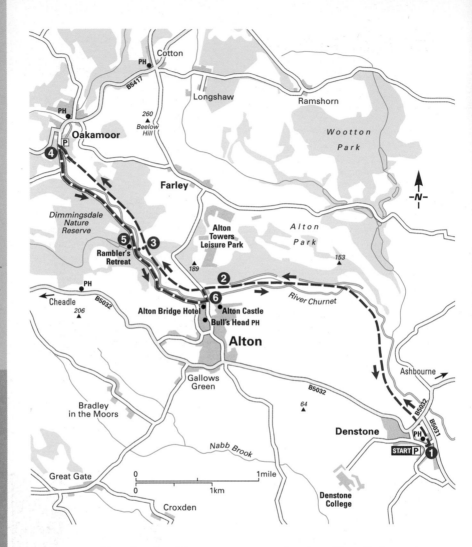

for many years. It's at the edge of the **Dimmingsdale Nature Reserve**, an area renowned for its variety of wild birds and woodland flowers.

5 You have a choice here. To regain the old railway take the gate opposite the car park entrance, cross the **Lord's Bridge** over the river and then the old railway bridge. Immediately left, walk your bike down to the trackbed and turn left beneath the bridge to

return to **Denstone**. Alternatively, remain on **Red Road**, tracing this along the foot of the gorge to reach the outskirts of **Alton**. Keep left to pass the **Alton Bridge Hotel**.

6 At the main road turn left and cross the river. At the sharp left bend, carefully cross to the right and take the potholed road beside an old factory to find a rough car park and the railway. Keep ahead to return to **Denstone**.

The Bull's Head

Traditional beers, home cooking and well-equipped accommodation are provided at the 300-year-old Bull's Head in the heart of Alton, less than a mile (1.6km) from Alton Towers Leisure Park. Oak beams, impressive wood panelling and an inglenook fireplace set the welcoming scene in the old-world bar, the cosy snug (where children can sit), and the country-style restaurant. Walls, beams and shelves are decorated with a wealth of bric-a-brac ranging from coal scuttles and old stone jars, to candlesticks, brasses and old local photographs. The pub is tucked away amid Georgian and medieval buildings – an area well worth exploring.

about the pub

The Bull's Head
High Street, Alton
Staffordshire ST10 4AQ
Tel 01538 702307
www.thebullsheadinn.co.uk

DIRECTIONS: from Denstone take the B5032 towards Cheadle. At a staggered junction on the edge of Alton take the road signed for Alton Towers. Drop down through the town to a sharp bend where High Street departs straight ahead. The Bull's Head is virtually at this junction

PARKING: 15

OPEN: daily, all day

FOOD: daily

BREWERY/COMPANY: free house

REAL ALE: Bass, Worthington Cask, Greene King, Abbot Ale

ROOMS: 7 bedrooms

Food

There's a new a la carte menu offering the likes of home-made steak and ale pie and Cajun chicken, and a lunchtime menu based around sandwiches and baguettes.

Family facilities

Families are made most welcome here; children can settle and relax in the snug bar where they have their own menu to choose from. Outdoor seating is limited to a few tables and chairs on a paved area.

Alternative refreshment stops

There are pubs in Oakamoor, Alton and Denstone. The Rambler's Retreat restaurant and café is on the route.

☛ Where to go from here

Visit Alton Towers Leisure Park (www.altontowers.com), or Sudbury Hall and Museum of Childhood, to the south east (www.nationaltrust.org).

Churnet Valley

STAFFORDSHIRE

Osmaston and Shirley

Follow challenging gravel roads and peaceful back lanes between charming medieval and estate villages near Ashbourne.

Shirley village

Shirley is the oldest of a gaggle of peaceful little villages visited on this ride. The village is recorded in the Domesday book; St Michael's Church originates from this period although it was rebuilt in Victorian times when the renowned Edwardian novelists, brothers John Cowper and Theodore Francis Powys, were born in the vicarage here. Note the enormous yew tree in the churchyard. At the edge of the village is Shirley Hall, family home to the Earls Ferrers.

The valley of Shirley Brook was dammed to power mills, of which the most spectacular is the glorious Osmaston Saw Mill. This is on your left at the foot of the first long, rough descent. The vast,

landscaped lake powered the overshot wheel that still survives beneath its imposing gable. The mill itself is a rather eccentric building built in 1845 for the owners of Osmaston Hall. The cedar-tree dotted parkland still contains the walled gardens, but the hall itself is no more. Osmaston village, built largely to house workers on the estate, is a charming mix of thatched cottages and picturesque houses and farms surrounding a village duck pond.

the ride

1 Ride uphill from the **Saracen's Head**, shortly passing by the gates to **St Michael's Church** at the heart of the village of Shirley. At the bend, fork left along the level lane, singposted **'No Through Road'**. This starts a very gradual climb away from the village. Beyond the sports ground, the lane becomes a rough track.

2 Keep left at the fork by the **brick barn**, starting a hill which courses along the

edge of a largely fir tree plantation. At the top a cross-track runs along the lip of a steep slope. Go ahead here down a very steep and loose gravel descent through beech woods into the valley of **Shirley Brook**. It levels off between a huge mill pond and the old **saw mill**, before commencing an equally challenging ascent through landscaped **Osmaston Park**. Keep ahead as the surface changes to tar and then back again, before reaching the valley crest above a spinney. Ride ahead from here to reach the village of **Osmaston**.

3 It's worth exploring this charming little village before returning to the duck pond and green. Put this on your left and take the road for **Wyaston** and **Yeaveley**. A level 0.5 miles (800m) follows, the typical higher hedges with banks of wild flowers lining the route. A descent into a shallow valley means a lengthy uphill stretch before the quiet, winding lane reaches the **Shire Horse Inn** at the edge of **Wyaston**. Keep on the main lane, soon entering this straggling hamlet. Pass by the first left turn and continue beyond the village to a second left turn (Shirley and Rodsley), also signed as **National Cycle Trail 68**. Turn left here and trace the lane all the way through to the cross lanes at the heart of **Rodsley**.

4 You have a choice of routes here. To cut the full route short, turn left at this crossroads and cycle the lane back to Shirley. It's an undulating lane with a long but gradual hill after **Shirley Mill Farm** as the final flourish into **Shirley** itself. For the

Top: The village pond in Osmaston
Left: Osmaston Saw Mill

3h30 · **10 MILES** · **16.1 KM** · **LEVEL 1 2 3**

SHORTER ALTERNATIVE ROUTE

2h30 · **6.75 MILES** · **10.9 KM** · **LEVEL 1 2 3**

MAP: OS Explorer 259 Derby

START/FINISH: Saracen's Head in Shirley (check with landlord beforehand for parking), grid ref SK220416

TRAILS/TRACKS: back lanes and rough tracks, one section of busier road on the longer option

LANDSCAPE: mixed arable and pasture farmland, country estates

PUBLIC TOILETS: none on route

TOURIST INFORMATION: Ashbourne, tel 01335 343666

CYCLE HIRE: nearest is on the Tissington Trail at Mapleton Lane, north of Ashbourne town centre, tel 01335 343156

THE PUB: The Saracen's Head, Shirley, see Point **1** on route

🚴 Some short, steep ascents and descents; high hedges along some roads. Some very challenging short hills, which will not suit younger children or less-fit cyclists. The longer option has a section of busier road, with good sight lines. Suitable for experienced family groups with older children who have road cycling experience

Getting to the start

Shirley is signposted off the A52 about 6 miles (9.6km) south east of Ashbourne.

Why do this cycle ride?

A web of quiet by-roads and single track lanes threads this peaceful area. The result is rewarding cycling amidst hay meadows, pastureland, woods and fields, with good views, and visits to several estate villages.

Researched and written by: Neil Coates

Shirley **DERBYSHIRE**

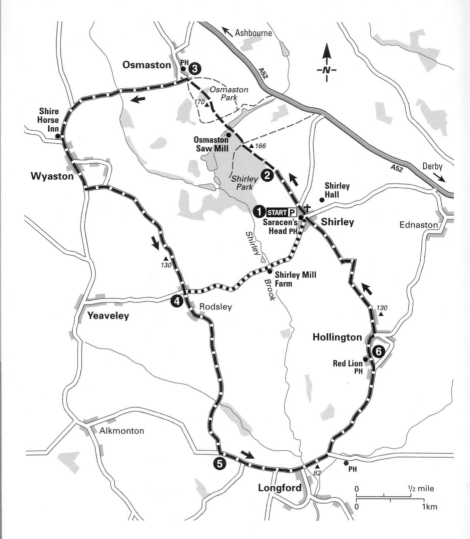

longer route, keep ahead at the crossroads, rising up through the hamlet along a narrowing lane to trace a winding course through to a T-junction with a busier road.

5 Turn left here along **Long Lane**. The road is easy riding, but take care as traffic is faster and much more common. Great views open out across south Derbyshire as you drop gradually into the valley of **Longford Brook**. In a mile (1.6km) turn left at a sign for

Hollington, starting a gradual climb up **Hoargate Lane**. At a junction with Back Lane, keep left up along **Main Street** and past the strand of houses and farms of **Hollington**.

6 Pass by the **Red Lion** and bend right to reach a cross lanes. Turn left along **Shirley Lane** (also Marsh Hollow), following this single track, partially green-centred lane through to **Shirley** village.

The Saracen's Head

Pub and church stand close together at the heart of this tiny, picturesque village. The pub (dated 1791) is an attractive white-painted brick building, with plants clambering up the walls and a tiny front garden filled with delphiniums. To the rear, outbuildings have been converted into letting cottages. Inside you'll find a single, L-shaped bar with a mix of tiled and carpeted floors, comfortable upholstered bench seating, and lovely views of rose-bedecked cottages and the churchyard. On tap you'll find a decent pint of Black Sheep Bitter and the menu lists some good, home-cooked food. It's a great village pub with few pretensions, an affable landlord and an easy-going atmosphere.

Food

The bar menu offers a good choice of contemporary home-cooked food, for example beef platter, fish and chips, penne pasta, chicken, bacon and mushroom pie and decent filled rolls. Blackboard specials might highlight a range of curries including Thai green chicken.

Family facilities

Small children can order smaller portions from the main menu. They can tuck into their meal in the pub or on fine days they can enjoy the flower-filled garden.

Alternative refreshment stops

Pubs at Osmaston (Shoulder of Mutton) and Wyaston (The Shire Horse).

☛ Where to go from here

Kedleston Hall is one of England's greatest country houses, built in 1765 when the entire village was moved to improve the owner's views (www.nationaltrust.org.uk).

about the pub

The Saracen's Head

Shirley, Ashbourne
Derbyshire DE6 3AS
Tel 01335 360330

DIRECTIONS: see Getting to the start

PARKING: 20. Please check beforehand with landlord before leaving your car in the car park

OPEN: closed Sunday evenings, all day Monday and Tuesday

FOOD: daily

BREWERY/COMPANY: Greene King

REAL ALE: IPA, Abbot and Speckled Hen

ROOMS: None available

Shirley **DERBYSHIRE**

The Shropshire Canal

With more miles of canal than any other county, what better way to discover Staffordshire's countryside?

Shropshire Canal

The Shropshire Canal was built between 1830 and 1835 under the direction of Thomas Telford, creating a more direct link than hitherto between the industrial towns of England's heartland and the seaports along the Dee and Mersey rivers. A branch from Norbury ran to Wappenshall Junction on the edge of Telford where, via the Shrewsbury Canal and the Hay Inclined Plane, boats could reach the ironworks and potteries of the Ironbridge Gorge. From the very beginning, canals proved their worth in moving heavy and bulky cargoes cheaply and quickly, and the late 18th and early 19th centuries saw a period of spectacular industrial growth as the network spread across the country. All operated on a system of tolls to cover the cost of construction and maintenance and there was intense competition between rival routes to attract trade. Junctions like that here at Norbury would have been controlled with a toll bar, where charges were levied on the type of goods and weight carried. There would also have been a certain amount of reloading too, as cargoes were split or combined for the various destinations served by the separate branches. Alongside the canals, inns, stables and blacksmiths sprang up to provide sustenance for the bargees and the horses that pulled the boats. Workyards were also necessary to undertake repairs on the barges as well as to provide depots for the gangs maintaining the canal itself.

The branch to Wappenshall and Telford fell into disuse during the 1930s, the trade having been taken over by the railways. By the end of the war, it had been completely abandoned and much of it was filled in. You can still trace its ghostly course on the map, where odd short stretches are shown as pools. The main Shropshire Canal

The Shropshire Canal at Gnosall Heath

A barge on the Shropshire Canal

1h30 — **6.5 MILES** — **10.6 KM** — **LEVEL 123**

MAP: Explorer 243 Market Drayton, Loggerheads & Eccleshall

START/FINISH: Norbury Village Hall; grid ref: SJ782235

TRAILS/TRACKS: canal towpath (one short grass section) and quiet lanes

LANDSCAPE: open countryside and woodland

PUBLIC TOILETS: none on route

TOURIST INFORMATION: Stafford, tel 01785 619619

CYCLE HIRE: none locally

THE PUB: The Navigation Inn, Gnosall

⚠ One main road crossing, two dark bridges, towpaths (can be muddy after rain)

Getting to the start

Norbury lies 8.5 miles (13.7km) west of Stafford. An unclassified road off the A519 3 miles (4.8km) north of Newport leads into the village.

Why do this cycle ride?

An easy uncomplicated ride along quiet and gently undulating country lanes to the village of Gnosall Heath, where there is a splendid canalside pub. The return is along the canal, often busy with colourful boats plying their way through the Heart of England.

Researched and written by: Dennis Kelsall

survived and is today busy with leisure boats and colourful painted barges. Set against the backdrop of buildings at Norbury Junction, it takes little imagination to envisage how the waterway might have looked during its heyday.

the ride

1 Out of the car park go right and then left to pedal through the village, signed to **Oulton and Norbury Junction**. Keep with the main lane as it bends right past a track leading to the striking village **church**, a large building, dedicated to St Peter, of much weathered sandstone that nestles below a massive brick tower. Leaving the village, go left at a fork signed to **Norbury Junction and Gnosall**.

2 You will be passing through **Norbury Junction** on the way back, so for the time being, carry on over the canal bridge and continue along the lane behind the old canal offices and **workshops**. Beside the lane is a **millennium boulder**, similar to one beside the village hall, an erratic stranded as the vast ice sheets that covered this part of the country melted at the end of the last ice age, some 10,000 years ago. Beyond **cottages**, the lane falls towards a wood, there bending sharply right to pass under a **bridge** (beware of traffic).

3 At the junction beyond, go left towards **Gnosall**, the lane rising gently along the base of a high **wooded embankment** upon which the canal runs. After a mile (1.6km), it twists beneath the canal once more (again watch out for traffic) and climbs to a bend beyond. Keep going with the undulating lane, eventually passing beneath a bridge that once carried the Stafford Newport Railway to a **T-junction** with the main road at the end.

4 Turn right, crossing the canal to find **The Navigation** on the right. If going to the pub, there are steps to the canal towpath from the car park, but an easier way lies down a **ramp** on the left-hand side of the road. Double back under the bridge and cycle away past the pub beside the canal, shortly going beneath the railway

again. The **bridge** here is very wide, the passage almost tunnel-like, not due to carrying several tracks, but because it is skewed across the canal. Such bridges were disproportionately expensive if built in brick or stone, and it was only the invention of the skew arch that allowed the bridge to be preserved within the width of the upper passage. Shortly emerging from a **cutting**, there are pleasing views across the open countryside. The way continues to **Shelmore Wood**, where there is a **stop lock**, a device inserted periodically along the canal for isolating individual sections so that they could be drained for maintenance. Carry on in trees for another 1.25 miles (2km) to **Norbury Junction**, there crossing a bridge over the abandoned Wappenshall Branch to reach **The Junction pub**.

5 Leave the canal for the lane, and retrace your outward route left back to the car park by the village hall in Norbury.

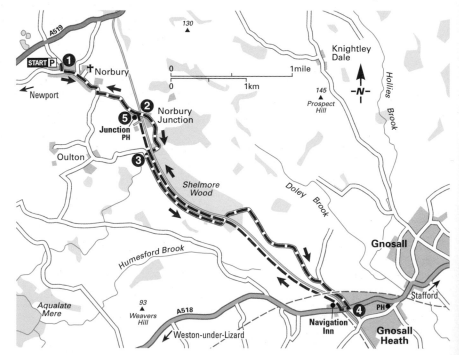

The Navigation Inn

Constructed to serve the needs of the workers building the Shropshire Canal in the 1830s, the Navigation is a traditional, cream-painted pub smack beside the canal, with several cosy rooms adorned with brassware. There's also an airy conservatory dining area which overlooks the garden and passing canal boats.

Food

Standard pub food is available, the snack menu listing ploughman's lunches and a good range of sandwiches. The a la carte menu extends the choice to include steak and kidney pie, jumbo haddock and lamb shank, while the specials board may add choices such as wild boar, liver and bacon and fresh fish dishes.

Family facilities

Families can expect a good welcome here as children are allowed throughout the pub. Youngsters have a standard children's menu and they will love exploring the play area in a canal-side garden.

Alternative refreshment stops

The Junction pub at Norbury Junction.

☞ Where to go from here

At Weston-under-Lizard you'll find Weston Park (www.weston-park.com), a fine mansion built in 1671. It stands in elegant gardens and a vast park with three lakes, a miniature railway, a woodland adventure playground, an animal centre and deer park. The house contains a magnificent collection of pictures, furniture and tapestries. Take a self-guided tour of the Wedgwood Ceramic Factory at Barlaston (www.wedgwood.com) and learn all about the story of the famous Wedgwood china. The visitor centre has a film theatre, exhibition area and a demonstration area with hands-on exhibits.

about the pub

The Navigation Inn
Newport Road, Gnosall
Staffordshire ST20 0BM
Tel: 01785 822327

DIRECTIONS: beside the canal and A518 Newport road just west of the village; Point **4** of the route

PARKING: 50

OPEN: daily; all day in summer

FOOD: daily; all day in summer

BREWERY/COMPANY: Punch Taverns

REAL ALE: Banks Bitter & Original, changing guest beer

Cannock Chase

Cycle around Britain's smallest Area of Outstanding Natural Beauty.

Cannock Chase

Today covering some 26 square miles (6,734ha), Cannock Chase was once part of a vast Norman Royal Forest, where severe penalties were meted out for encroachment and poaching. By the end of the 13th century, the hunting rights had been granted to the Bishop and soon parts of the domain were being enclosed within private estates. By the 15th century, charcoal burners were coppicing the trees, producing fuel to smelt iron, and later large areas were cleared, with sheep being loosed onto the bare heaths. Coal mining began in the 17th century, developing rapidly as the canals arrived around the Chase's perimeter and continuing until the last century.

During World War I, two large infantry training camps were established on the Chase and later, a German prisoner of war camp was opened. There was also a hospital to treat the wounded brought back from France and which was inundated when an influenza epidemic struck the country just after the war ended in 1918. Many tragically died from the illness and are buried in the Commonwealth War Cemetery near Broadhurst Green, whilst next to it is the German War Cemetery, opened in 1967 and in which most of the Germans who died in this country during both wars are now buried.

The extensive forest area encourages a great diversity of wildlife, and amongst the animals you might see are three of the six species of deer to be found in Britain: fallow, red and the tiny muntjack. There are also foxes, badgers, hares and of course rabbits, with plenty of squirrels, both grey and red. On warm sunny days you may spot an adder or common lizard, whilst in the trees, are cuckoos, green woodpeckers and jays.

the ride

1 Leave the main car park at a large **signpost** to pass the District Office, turning left on a wide drive in front of Swinnerton's **cycle hire centre**. Immediately beyond, look for a track on the right marked '**Fairoak Walk**', which leads eventually to a T-junction. Go right, dropping around a left-hand bend to a second junction. Swing right again, the way still marked 'Fairoak Walk', passing a small **pond** to a fork at the edge of a clearing. Go left and then left again, a little further on, to skirt a **larger pool**. Meeting a broad track go right and then at its end, turn left.

2 Keep ahead past a track to **fishing lakes** on the right, soon reaching another junction. Turn right to climb through a **pine plantation**, meeting a cross-track after the gradient eases. To the right, another steep pull leads to a fork, where you should keep left, dropping sharply to another crossing. Go left, the way undulating more easily and eventually reaching a T-junction. Turn right onto **Marquis Drive**, passing the Park Rangers' depot and then emerging through a **gate**.

3 The **visitor centre** and toilets are off to the left, but the route continues ahead to a lane. Follow it right to a crossroads at **Flints Corner**, where the ongoing path

Woods in Sherbrook Valley, Cannock Chase

3h30 — **13.2 MILES** — **21.2 KM** — **LEVEL 123**

marked **'Heart of England Way'** lies ahead, just to the right of the lane facing you. Go into the trees, soon reaching a crossing track. Turn right and then almost immediately left, doing the same at the next crossing, a little further on, to meet a road.

4 Cross to the continuing path opposite, which drops at the edge of **heather heath**. At a T-junction bear left to continue into the head of **Sherbrook Valley**. Go forward at the first crossing, but then immediately swing right onto a broad stony track, marked as the **cycleway**. A long descent hugs the base of the fold, loosely following the brook from which it takes its name. Part-way down, the track doglegs as another gully comes in from the left, resuming its course to pass a **small wood and pools**. Eventually, after a good 2 miles (3.2km) of cycling, go right at a junction, crossing the stream at a **ford**. Pedal on along an undulating track, finally bearing left at a fork to arrive at the **Beggar's Hill car park**.

5 Turn sharp right, doubling back onto a narrower path that rises gently into **Abraham's Valley**. Where it divides, keep right, climbing more steeply for a while until you reach a broad crossing track. Go right past an open area of younger trees and stay ahead across another wide track onto a narrower gravel way. Shortly, at a **5-way junction**, where just ahead is a **trig point**, turn left, now running easily along the high point of the ride. Continue forward at a later fork, eventually dropping to a T-junction near some **buildings**. Cycling left through a car park, then right, leave along a wide gravel road.

MAP: OS Explorer 6 Cannock Chase and Chasewater

START/FINISH: Birches Valley Forest Centre; grid ref: SK018171

TRAILS/TRACKS: forest tracks throughout

LANDSCAPE: hilly woodland and heath

PUBLIC TOILETS: at Birches Valley Forest Centre and Cannock Chase Visitor Centre

TOURIST INFORMATION: Stafford, tel 01785 619619

THE PUB: The Horns Inn, Slitting Mill

CYCLE HIRE: at start – Swinnerton Cycles, Forest Enterprise, Birches Valley, Lady Hill, Rugeley, tel 01889 575170, www.swinnertoncycles.co.uk

🛑 Road crossings, loose gravel tracks, some overhanging branches, track shared with pedestrians and horses. Some hills with occasional attention to route finding – for older, more experienced children

Getting to the start

Birch Valley Forest Centre is 2 miles (3.2km) west of Rugeley. Take a minor road to Slitting Mill and bear right at a fork approaching the village onto Cannock Chase. The centre is signed to the left.

Why do this cycle ride?

A route with plenty of ups and downs that will appeal to adventurous families. The ride reveals many different facets of the Chase, from plantations to natural woodland and open heath. The area abounds in wildlife.

Researched and written by: Dennis Kelsall

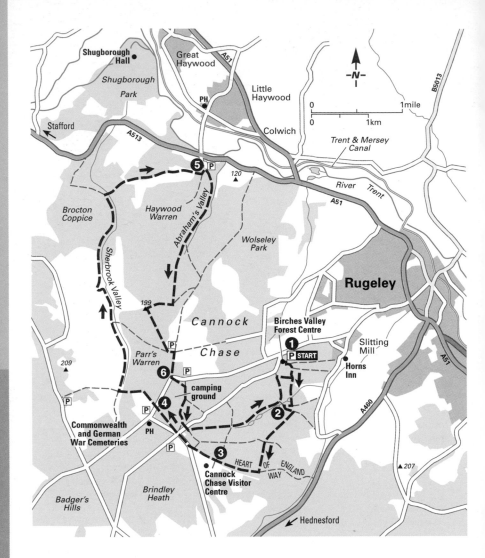

6 Meeting the main road at **Rifle Range Corner**, carefully cross to a bridleway opposite. At the end bear right on a broad track, and then branch right again to pedal through a **camping area**. Keep ahead at the far side on a narrower path, gently descending through the trees. At a waymarked junction, go left, following **green and orange markers** out to another road. Cross to a barriered track opposite,

almost immediately bearing left into a steadily steepening valley. Keep ahead over a bridleway past **Fairoak Pools**, then at the bottom, go left, climbing to the crest of the rise. Turn off right across a more open area to a crossing track at the far side and bear left and then left again past a **small pond**. The way back to the start point lies along to the left, retracing your outward route to the Forest Centre.

The Horns Inn

Slitting Mill village takes its name from the type of work the mills carried out along the stream, the process of splitting (slitting) wood and metal. Dating back around 200 years, the Horns is a brick-built pub that has been modernised and extended over the years, resulting in a large bar and open-plan dining areas. The atmosphere is bright and cheerful, there are some cosy corners tucked away by the bar, old pictures of the pub on the walls, and the staff are friendly and welcoming. Super summer patio adorned with colourful flower baskets.

Food
The menu has three sections. There's a choice of steaks, chicken with Stilton and lamb shanks from the a la carte menu, steak au poivre and crepes Suzette from the flambé menu or a selection of fish specials such as halibut, seabass, grilled hake and grilled prawns.

Family facilities
Children are welcome in the pub and there is a children's menu for younger family members.

Alternative refreshment stops
Light refreshments at Birches Valley Forest Centre and a café at Cannock Chase Visitor Centre.

☞ Where to go from here
Head for Shugborough Hall (www.shugborough.org.uk) on the edge of Cannock Chase. A fine 18th-century mansion, set in 900 magnificent acres, containing fine collections of ceramics, silver, paintings and French furniture. At Whittington you can visit the Staffordshire Regiment Museum, where exhibits include vehicles, uniforms, weapons, medals and memorabilia relating to 300 years of regimental history, and visitors can also experience a World War I trench system with sound effects (www.staffordshireregimentmuseum.com).

about the pub

The Horns Inn
Slitting Mill Road, Slitting Mill
Rugeley, Staffordshire WS15 2UW
Tel: 01889 586000

DIRECTIONS: load up bikes, turn right out of the car park and right again to the village. At a junction there, go sharp right again to reach the pub.

PARKING: 50

OPEN: daily; all day Saturday & Sunday

FOOD: daily

BREWERY/COMPANY: Punch Taverns

REAL ALE: Marston's Pedigree, Tetley, guest beer

Along the Ashby Woulds Heritage Trail

Celebrate Leicestershire's rich industrial heritage on this short linear cycle ride along the track of a disused railway line.

Ashby Woulds Heritage Trail

The Ashby Woulds Heritage Trail follows the route of the old Ashby to Nuneaton railway, and runs right through the heart of what was once an important coal-mining area. When pits were closed across the region in the mid 1980s, the landscape was left derelict and decaying, but in 1992 a forum was formed to help regenerate the local environment and boost the region's economy. The trail is a part of this initiative. It starts at the old railway station in Measham before crossing Donisthorpe Woodland Park, which was planted on the site of a reclaimed colliery. Further along is Conkers, a state-of-the-art visitor centre built on the site of Rawdon Colliery, one of the last deep mines in the Midlands to close. It finishes at Overseal sidings, where a short length of track and an abandoned signal box can still be seen. The trail also falls within the so-called National Forest, a government-backed initiative instigated in 1995 to help improve some 200 square miles of land in Leicestershire, Derbyshire and Staffordshire which have been scarred by hundreds of years of coal mining. It is hoped that 30 million trees will eventually be planted, and that 33 per cent of the total area will be wooded.

Right: A pond on the Ashby Woulds Trail

the ride

1 From the south west corner of the car park, proceed up a narrow path to reach the main bridleway, past a **heritage trail information board**. Bear right along the gravel bridleway, past a **picnic bench** at the top of the rise. After 750yds (686m), the bridleway veers to the left and goes through some **wooden bike stiles** to reach a main road. At the main road turn right along the pavement and go under the **A42**.

2 Straight after the A42, turn right to regain the **main bridleway** (there is another right turn just before this which also looks like a bridleway, but this is clearly a dead end). Continue under a pair of **road bridges**. Much of this section, and indeed the whole trail, is raised up above the surrounding landscape, but because it's enclosed by trees and bushes, it feels quite secluded and peaceful. There are numerous **signposts** and **picnic benches** along the route.

3 Just beyond the next bridge, bear left up the first short climb of the ride to reach a **main road**. Turn right along the pavement and then cross the road with care to continue along the **heritage trail** (signed). Here the trail is wider and more open as it crosses **Donisthorpe Woodland Park**. On the way it drops down a long gentle hill to a bridge and a small stream before heading back up the far side.

4 At the northern corner of the park, keep going in the same direction (frustratingly enough, you may have to dismount here to negotiate a pair of **wooden bike stiles**). The trail becomes enclosed and shaded again

1h30 — **6.8 MILES** — **11 KM** — **LEVEL 123**

MAP: OS Explorer 245 The National Forest

START/FINISH: Measham Country Park car park; grid ref SK332119

TRAILS/TRACKS: mostly gravel, with a short section of pavement

LANDSCAPE: railway embankment

PUBLIC TOILETS: at the start

TOURIST INFORMATION: Ashby-de-la-Zouch, tel 01530 411767

CYCLE HIRE: none locally

THE PUB: Navigation Inn, Overseal

❶ Take care when riding along the pavement under the A42, and also when crossing the road in Donisthorpe. Keep an eye on young children when approaching the road at the Navigation Inn

Getting to the start

Park at a free car park just off the B5006 in the middle of Measham, which is signposted off the A42 1.5 miles (2km) south west of Ashby-de-la-Zouch. Go to the left-hand parking area, where the public toilets are situated.

Why do this cycle ride?

This gentle ride is almost completely flat, and what it lacks in terms of views it more than makes up for in terms of peace and solitude. The family-friendly pub at the halfway point is an ideal spot for a rest, and kids will love the attractions at Conkers Visitor Centre, a short detour off the main route.

Researched and written by: Paul Grogan

Measham LEICESTERSHIRE

On the Ashby Woulds Trail

as you pass over a number of roads before eventually getting to a string of **ponds** at the end of the trail; just beyond these ponds is the B5004 and, off to your left, **the Navigation Inn**.

5 To reach the **National Forest Visitor Centre (Conkers)**, go back along the trail and at the far end of the **ponds** turn left, following a sign to the **Bath Yard**. When you come to another **sign** and information board turn right, into a field, and cross it on

a well-trodden track. Turn right at the far end of this track, under a bridge, and continue as far as a **railway crossing**. Just beyond this crossing is the visitor centre.

6 To get back to the start, retrace your tracks from the Navigation Inn or the visitor centre. At the main road in Donisthorpe turn right and then left to stay on route, and at the main road into **Measham**, turn left along the pavement to go under the A42 and then left again, back into the woods.

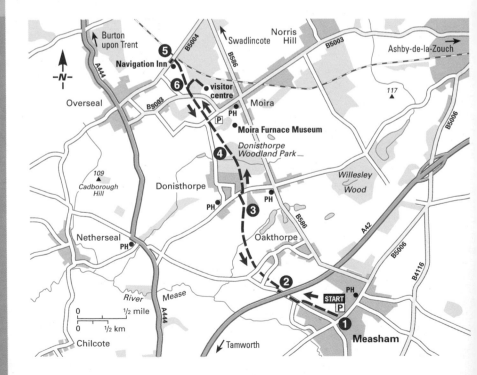

Measham LEICESTERSHIRE

Navigation Inn

Interesting black and white prints of the local area adorn the walls of this big, family-orientated pub situated in Overseal village. Both the bar and dining areas are open-plan in layout, light, spacious and immaculately maintained, and decorated in traditional style with dark wood tables and chairs laid out on bright red carpets. In the summer the big garden is very popular with families and children are able to let off steam in the huge adventure play area.

Food

An extensive menu offers light meals like sandwiches, wraps and paninis, standard pub main courses, and dishes like lasagne, steak and ale pie and chicken in white wine sauce, all served with freshly prepared vegetables or salad.

Family facilities

Children of all ages are welcome throughout the pub and there's a safe, enclosed adventure play area in the large lawned garden. There's a children's menu or smaller portions from the main menu.

Alternative refreshment stops

There's a café at Conkers that serves hot and cold drinks, snacks and main meals throughout the day.

☛ Where to go from here

Aside from Conkers, other local attractions worth visiting include the superb Moira Furnace Museum, just off the route, which boasts a host of displays and interactive exhibits on the history of the furnace, and Ashby Castle in Ashby-de-la-Zouch, which offers great views of the surrounding countryside. There's also a dry-slope ski centre in nearby Swadlincote just 3km (2 miles) to the north of the Navigation Inn (www.jnll.co.uk).

about the pub

Navigation Inn
166 Spring Cottage Road, Overseal
Swadlincote, Derbyshire DE12 6ND
Tel: 01283 760493

DIRECTIONS: on B5004 east of Overseal (Point 5 on the route)	
PARKING: 50	
OPEN: daily; all day Friday-Sunday	
FOOD: daily; not Monday	
BREWERY/COMPANY: Hardy & Hanson's	
REAL ALE: Hardy & Hanson's Bitter, Marston's Pedigree	
ROOMS: 2 bedrooms	

Measham LEICESTERSHIRE

Around Rutland Water

Ride around Europe's largest man-made reservoir at the heart of England's smallest county.

Rutland Water

Rutland Water was rubber-stamped in 1970 to provide drinking water to the surrounding area. Completed seven years later, it flooded an area of 3,100 acres (equivalent to around 3,000 football pitches). The dam itself is 1,312yds (1,200m) long, and the maximum depth of the reservoir is 34 metres (111ft). One of the few local landmarks to survive the flooding was Normanton Church, which had to be raised above the level of the water and joined to the shore by a causeway to protect it from ruin. Originally built in 1826, it today houses a local history museum. Other attractions include a climbing wall and marina (at Whitwell car park), a butterfly centre (at the north end of the dam), and a nature reserve (at the southwest corner of the reservoir).

The nature reserve is one of the most important bird-watching centres in the UK. Depending on the time of year, Rutland Water is home to as many as 20,000 waterfowl. Equally important are the reserve's ospreys. These impressive raptors have brown plumage, white bodies and wingspans of up to 5.6ft (1.7m). They were introduced to the region in 1996 in an attempt to encourage them to start breeding, and in 2003, after a few false starts, the ospreys were successfully bred in England for the first time since 1847. The reserve also boasts an environmental display, a viewing gallery, 22 hides and a nature trail.

the ride

1 From the car park exit opposite the bike shop and **climbing tower**, turn right and then immediately left into the **marina**. Follow the road round to the left, away from the marina buildings, and drop down to the water's edge as it becomes a **cycle track**. Turn right at the tip of the inlet and continue around the **water's edge** until you reach another car park. Continue through this car park to reach the dam.

2 After crossing the **dam**, turn right at the end, through a pair of swing gates, and continue along the obvious tarmac track as far as **Normanton Church**. Beyond the church, cross a narrow tarmac road and continue straight through an uneven gravel parking area to reach the main **Edith Weston car park**, with public toilets, snack bar and bike shop. Proceed to the far end of the car park and turn right to continue around the water's edge, past the **sailing club** and marina.

An undulating path near Rutland Water

3h00 — **17 MILES** — **27.4 KM** — **LEVEL 1 2 3**

MAP: OS Explorer 234 Rutland Water

START/FINISH: Whitwell car park; grid ref: SK923082

TRAILS/TRACKS: largely smooth tarmac and compacted gravel and tarmac

LANDSCAPE: woodland and waterside, with the occasional village

PUBLIC TOILETS: at the start and at Edith Weston car park

TOURIST INFORMATION: Oakham, tel 01572 724329

CYCLE HIRE: Rutland Cycling (at the start), tel 01780 460705 (www.rutlandcycling.co.uk)

THE PUB: The White Horse, Empingham

🛑 There's one short, steep descent with a tight turn at the bottom (well signposted). Take care crossing the main road when you make the right turn towards Manton

Getting to the start

The north and south shores of Rutland Water are signed from the A606 between Oakham and Stamford. This route starts at Whitwell car park on the north shore. Coming from Stamford, drive through Whitwell and turn left at the top of the hill to the car park.

Why do this cycle ride?

This is a long but gentle circuit that mostly follows the water's edge. The first few miles of tarmac are ideal for younger children, while the tracks on the western half are great for older, more adventurous kids. You can walk the one or two short sharp ascents.

Researched and written by: Paul Grogan

3 A mile (1.6km) past the sailing club, the track delves into a small **wood** before dropping down a steep hill to a **tight bend** at the bottom; a sign near the top gives riders plenty of warning that this hill is coming up.

4 At the next road turn left up a steep hill to reach the B-road between **Edith Weston and Manton**. Cross the main road with care and then turn right towards Manton, following the **cycle lane**. At the first junction continue straight on into Manton. Soon after passing a **phone box** on your left, turn right, following a **Rutland Water cycling sign**. Bear left past the **Horse & Jockey** pub to reach a wide gravel track down to the A6003. Follow a narrow pavement at the bottom beneath the **railway bridge** (a sign advises riders to dismount for this bit) and stay on this pavement for a further 440yds (402m).

5 Turn right through a **swing gate** here, following the cycle track around the water's edge until it cuts across the Lax-Hill

Rutland Water **RUTLAND**

81

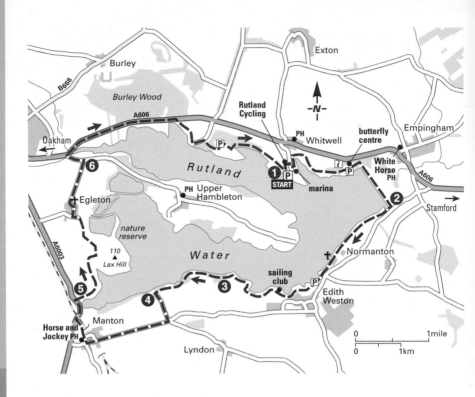

peninsula. This track eventually leads to **Egleton**. Make a left turn into the village and then turn right again after around 200yds (182m). Continue cycling past the **church** and stay on the road to the main road into Hambleton.

6 Turn left, and then right after 300yds (273m) along a short **cycle track** to reach the A606. From here, stay on the rolling pavement for 1.5 miles (2km), before heading right, back onto a gravel track and around the water's edge. At the bottom of the next tarmac road, turn left up the short, sharp hill before turning right towards **Barnsdale Wood car park**. After going down and then steeply uphill to reach the car park, continue downhill again to the bottom far right-hand corner of the car park; delve into **Barnsdale Wood** here and follow the track all the way back to the start point.

Modern sculpture above Rutland Water

The White Horse

A stone's throw from the serene Rutland Water, the stone-built, 17th-century White Horse is the centre of village life and a meeting place for the walkers, cyclists, anglers and water-sport enthusiasts exploring Europe's largest man-made lake. Originally a court house, it is now a popular inn with smart accommodation, a restaurant and a genteel, country-style bar, the latter full of traditional character, with low, beamed ceilings, dark wooden furniture and a large open log fire for cold winter days. In attempting to be all things to most callers its day stretches from morning coffee and croissants through lunches and cream teas to late evening suppers.

Food
Daily blackboard and printed menus typically include giant Yorkshire pudding filled with sautéed liver of lamb, bacon and onions, beef, ale and mushroom pie, and trout with prawns, mixed pepper and spring onion sauce. Lighter meals include soups, moules and pasta dishes.

Family facilities
Children of all ages are welcome. There's a children's menu and smaller portions are also available. Small sheltered garden and two family bedrooms.

Alternative refreshment stops
Drinks, ice-creams and hot and cold snacks are available from the café at the Edith Weston Car Park. Another pub on route is the Horse & Jockey in Manton.

☞ Where to go from here
About 10 miles (16.1km) to the east of Rutland Water, on the B1443 out of Stamford, is Burghley House, a great Elizabethan palace surrounded by a fine country park landscaped by Capability Brown (www.burghley.co.uk). Head east to Oakham to view the town's castle, an exceptionally fine Norman Great Hall of a 12th-century fortified manor house. Earthworks, walls and remains of an earlier motte can be seen along with medieval sculptures. Learn more about England's smallest county by visiting the Rutland County Museum in Catmos Street.

about the pub

The White Horse
2 Main Street, Empingham
Stamford, Rutland LE15 8PS
Tel: 01780 460221
www.whitehorserutland.co.uk

DIRECTIONS: load up bikes, return to Whitwell and turn right along the A606 for 2 miles (3.2km) to Empingham. The pub is at the junction with the main village street

PARKING: 60

OPEN: daily; all day

FOOD: daily; all day Sunday

BREWERY/COMPANY: Enterprise Inns

REAL ALE: Ruddles Best, Adnams Bitter, Greene King Abbot Ale

ROOMS: 13 en suite

The Silkin Way to Ironbridge

Pedal back in time to discover what a 'Saggar-maker's Bottom Knocker' did!

Coalbrookdale

Although the gorge's natural resources had been exploited since medieval times, the industrial boom only began here in 1709 with Abraham Darby's invention at Coalbrookdale that used coke rather than charcoal to produce large quantities of cast iron cheaply. It was his grandson who was responsible for the graceful cast-iron bridge that spans the gorge, erected between 1777 and 1779. Its 400 tons of castings represented nearly 4 months' output from a blast furnace and was the first structure of its kind to be erected.

But it was not only the blast of iron furnaces that lit up the gorge, for the abundant clay deposits in the area spawned a massive ceramic industry, with tile, pottery and china factories being set up beside the river. Indeed, Coalport was the new town of its day, established to house the families working in the potteries. To service the industries, a canal was built to Shrewsbury in 1793, with a link being built later to Norbury that gave access to the Shropshire Canal, some 18 miles (29km) away. In such hilly country, the use of locks was totally impractical, but William Reynolds, who owned ironworks here, invented the inclined plane whereby the tub-like boats could be lowered and raised on tracks between the different levels.

The most spectacular example is the Hay Inclined Plane, which moved the boats a vertical distance of over 200 feet (61m) in a matter of minutes, an operation that would otherwise have taken hours had the equivalent 27 locks been used.

The railways inevitably followed, the LNWR branch to Coalport (now the Silkin Way) being built in 1861 and the Severn Valley Railway the year after. A large goods yard grew up at Jackfield where coal, pottery, iron, tar and many other commodities were marshalled for transport to the various industrial centres and seaports around the country. Yet, even the railways lasted barely a century, for the decline had set in long before Beeching recommended his

Left: The cast-iron bridge that spans the gorge and the River Severn at Coalbrookdale

sweeping cuts to the rail system, as a result of under-investment after the War and competition from the greater flexibility offered by road transport.

the ride

1 Leaving the car park, cross the road and climb shallow steps to a tarmac track, the **Silkin Way**. Follow it left, passing **Station Road** and dropping to curve beneath the main road. Swing right as you emerge and carry on at the edge of a **park**, later joining the pavement to reach **Blists Hill Victorian Town**. Keep going down the hill, the cycleway shortly diverging from the road on a gradual tree-lined descent along the line of an old railway. Through a **short tunnel**, the way courses enjoyably down, later passing beneath the ingenious **Hay Inclined Plane**. The track eventually ends in front of the **Brewery Inn**.

2 Cross the road to a gated track left of the pub, that descends past **cottages** to the **riverbank**. Bear right as it forks, rising to meet a road. Follow that over the Severn, and then leave immediately down **steps** on the right to reach a riverside path. It skirts a **picnic area** and climbs around to a gate, there joining the line of another disused railway. The track continues above the river for just over half a mile (800m) before passing **Maws Craft Centre**, once the site of a booming tile industry. A little further on as the track ends, keep ahead on the right-most of two roads, which leads past more tile works at **Jackfield**. These were built by

2h00	7.5 MILES	12.1 KM	LEVEL 1 2 3

MAP: OS Explorer 242 Telford, Ironbridge & The Wreakin

START/FINISH: Legge Road car park, Madeley; grid ref: SJ700043

TRAILS/TRACKS: off-road tracks (can be muddy) and lanes, gentle descents and gradual climbs

LANDSCAPE: wooded valley

PUBLIC TOILETS: main car park at Blists Hill, at Maws Craft Centre and in Ironbridge

TOURIST INFORMATION: Ironbridge, tel 01952 884391

CYCLE HIRE: none locally

THE PUB: The Swan, Ironbridge

🚲 Although an easy ride, there are long, but gentle gradients, an unlit tunnel, short stretches of loose pebbles, steps, and some poorly surfaced roads

Getting to the start

Ironbridge Gorge lies south of Telford New Town. From the M54, follow the A442 south for 3 miles (4.8km), to its junction with the A4169. Turn right for Madeley, then at a roundabout as you approach the town, go left towards Blists Hill, Coalport and the Ironbridge Gorge Museums. The entrance to the car park is a short way along on the left.

Why do this cycle ride?

The gorge's tranquillity is deceptive, for here began a world-changing revolution. The ride takes you past the spectacular remains of its once-booming industry.

Researched and written by: Dennis Kelsall

Coalbrookdale

SHROPSHIRE

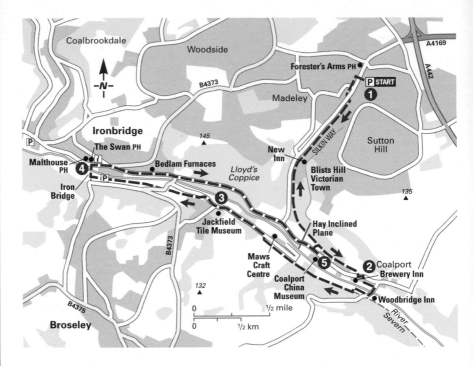

Charles Lynam between 1871 and 1874 for Craven Dunnill & Co. and now house a fascinating museum.

3 Go forward at a **junction**, but as the road then bends to a reconstructed level crossing, turn off left to regain the line of the railway through **Jackfield Sidings**. Further on, beyond the Black Swan, pass beneath a skew bridge carrying the road to the **Jackfield suspension bridge**. It is then not far to the main car park at Ironbridge. Pedal through to the far side and dismount to cross the famous **Iron Bridge** into the town, where you will find the Malthouse a little way to the left.

4 The route from the bridge, however, is along the main street to the right. At a mini-roundabout, take the right fork ahead, the B4373 to **Jackfield and Broseley**, leaving the town past the ruins of the

Bedlam Furnaces. Where the road later bends to Jackfield Bridge, keep ahead on a narrow, bumpy lane, which undulates along the valley to **Coalport**. Keep going forward at a later junction, a bridge taking you over the **Hay Inclined Plane**, just beyond which, opposite the Shakespeare Inn, you will find the entrance to the **Tar Museum**. A little further on is the **Coalport China Museum**.

5 From the museum, go back along the lane a few yards/metres, turning off right onto a track that winds around **Coalport Village Hall** to an overflow car park. Pass through it, right, to find a track climbing to meet the **Silkin Way**. Turn left and retrace your outward route past **Blists Hill** to the car park from which you began. The way is steadily uphill, but the track is well-graded and the climb relatively easy.

Right: A character in Blists Victorian Town

The Swan

An 18th-century former malthouse set on the riverfront close to the heart of Ironbridge. This was an inn during Darby's time and it is rumoured that site meetings were held at The Swan from time to time. The inn has been developed in recent years by Malthouse Pubs to create a modern pub but with traditional home-cooked food, a buzzy all-day bar, a summer courtyard, and a warm welcome.

Food

Expect a varied menu of freshly prepared dishes from around the world. Examples might be crispy aromatic duck, oyster beef and Californian salad or more substantial main meals such as braised lamb shank, bubble & squeak with port and redcurrant sauce, Cajun beefburger, and wild mushroom and basil risotto.

Family facilities

Children are welcome throughout the pub. There's a children's menu and smaller portions of adult dishes are also available.

Alternative refreshment stops

Along the way you have the Foresters' Arms at Madeley, a café at the entrance to Blists Hill Victorian Town and at Maws Craft Centre and pubs and cafés in Ironbridge.

☞ Where to go from here

There is so much to see and do as the whole area here is a World Heritage Site with a remarkable series of nine museums relating the story of the bridge, re-creating Victorian times and featuring ceramics and social history displays. Explore Blists Hill Victorian Town, the Museum of the Gorge, Coalport China Museum, Jackfield Tile Museum, the Museum of Iron, and the Broseley Pipeworks, among others (www.ironbridge.org.uk).

about the pub

The Swan
The Wharfage, Ironbridge
Shropshire, TF8 7NH
Tel: 01952 432306

DIRECTIONS: just east of the Iron Bridge, see Point **4**

PARKING: 10

OPEN: daily; all day

FOOD: daily; all day

BREWERY/COMPANY: free house

REAL ALE: 4 changing guest beers

ROOMS: 13 en suite

Coalbrookdale SHROPSHIRE

The Staffordshire & Worcestershire Canal

Explore two transport systems that spurred Britain's Industrial Revolution.

Staffordshire & Worcestershire Canal

The Staffordshire & Worcester Canal was engineered by James Brindley, and runs for 46 miles (74km) from Great Heywood Junction on the Trent & Mersey Canal to the River Severn at Stourport. Construction took six years and the canal opened in the year that Brindley died, 1772. It followed contours wherever possible, but still had to descend over 360 feet (110m) through 43 locks, one for almost every mile (1.6km).

The three at Bratch lower the canal 30 feet (9m) and are overlooked by an unusual turret toll house. A major cargo was coal from Staffordshire, a trade that continued into the 1940s.

The canals declined because of the faster transport offered by the railways, but the line here was never the success that had been anticipated. A branch-line off the Worcester to Wolverhampton railway, it opened in 1925 and serviced local coal and ironworkings. Passenger trains were rarely busy, and by 1932 had been withdrawn, although freight traffic continued for another 30 years until final closure in 1966. Today, the trackside has become a wildlife corridor along which woodland has been re-established, with birch, oak, alder and hawthorn forming a thick coppice. Many small birds find cover in the trees; redwings, redpolls, siskins, willow warblers and chiff chaffs, whilst hunting birds such as owls, kestrels and buzzards can sometimes be spotted. Small mammals such as voles and mice scurry about in the undergrowth, but there are foxes and badgers to be seen too.

the ride

1 Leave the car park at its far end to join the **disused railway track** and go along it to the right. After initial views across the fields the embankment becomes cloaked in trees and shrubs, the line passing beneath or over several bridges to reach the site of a former station, **Penn Halt**. Beneath more bridges, there is a long section through a wooded cutting, then a couple of barriers take the way across the end of a road connecting to a **housing estate**. Keep going, shortly passing the overgrown brickwork of a **platform** beside the path. Some 0.33 mile (500m) further on, and about 50yds (46m) before reaching a bridge at **Compton**, leave the embankment, dropping along a sloping path on the left to reach the main road at the foot of the bridge.

2h00 | **9 MILES** | **14.5 KM** | **LEVEL 1**23

2 Turn left over the **canal** and cross the road to the towpath access. Double back beneath the bridge and follow the bank away from Compton. In contrast to the railway path that was largely shrouded in trees, the canal offers more **open views** across the surrounding countryside, whilst bordering the bank here on the opposite side is a small **nature reserve**. After passing a couple of locks the way arrives at **Wightwick Bridge**.

3 The charming pre-Raphaelite **Wightwick Manor** (National Trust) lies close by, and although its hours of opening are limited, is well worth a visit. To get there, leave the canal as you emerge from the bridge, doubling back up to the road above. Turn left and, at the **traffic lights**, continue ahead over the main road beside **The Mermaid**, climbing a steepish hill to the entrance, some 100yds (91m) along on the left. Return to the canal and carry on, passing beneath successive bridges and eventually reaching **Dimingsdale Lock**.

4 The towpath now switches to the other bank, running down to **Awbridge Lock**, which is overlooked by an unusual bridge, its parapets decorated with brick balustrades, apparently a novel attempt by Brindley to combine lock and bridge in a single entity. Carry on to **Bratch Locks**, where the towpath reverts to the west bank above an impressive flight of locks, overlooked by a striking **octagonal toll house**.

5 Dismounting, re-cross the canal and wheel your bike down beside the locks.

Left and above: Cycling on the towpath of the Staffordshire and Worcestershire Canal

MAP: OS Explorer 219 Wolverhampton & Dudley

START/FINISH: Kingswinford Railway Path car park, Wombourne; grid ref: SO870940

TRAILS/TRACKS: well-surfaced track and towpath

LANDSCAPE: disused railway and canal through gentle countryside

PUBLIC TOILETS: none on route

TOURIST INFORMATION: Wolverhampton, tel 01902 556110

CYCLE HIRE: none locally

THE PUB: The Round Oak, Wombourne

⚠ Awkward barriers along railway track, low bridges and towpath occasionally narrow; children must be carefully supervised

Getting to the start

Wombourne lies 4 miles (6.4km) south west of Wolverhampton. Leave the A449 at its roundabout junction with the A463 along an unclassified road to Wombourne and the Kingswinford Railway Walk. Go ahead at a crossroads and continue for 0.6 mile (1.1km) to a car park signed off on the right.

Why do this cycle ride?

Many disused railway lines have found new life as footpaths and cycle tracks; the one at Wombourne, beside a canal, is an easy, off-road circular route. The return passes not far from Wightwick Manor, a fine mansion whose design and furnishing was greatly influenced by the Arts and Crafts Movement.

Researched and written by: Dennis Kelsall

Wombourne **WEST MIDLANDS**

If you want to return to the car park, you can leave via the lane and go left. The entrance to the **car park** lies 0.25 mile (400m) along, on the left immediately after **Bratch railway bridge**. Otherwise, carry on beside the canal beneath the road. After the last of the Bratch Locks has been passed through you can remount, continuing for a further 0.5 mile (800m) past **Bumblehole Lock** to a canalside pub, **The Round Oak** at Ounsdale Bridge.

6 Return along the canal to Bratch Locks and, joining the road, go right back to the car park. Notice on the right, as you leave Bratch Locks, a splendid polychrome brick building, looking more like a minor French chateau than an industrial building. It is, in fact, a **Victorian waterworks**, opened in 1897 to coincide with the queen's silver jubilee, and housed two steam driven pumps named in royal honour, 'Victoria' and 'Alexandra'.

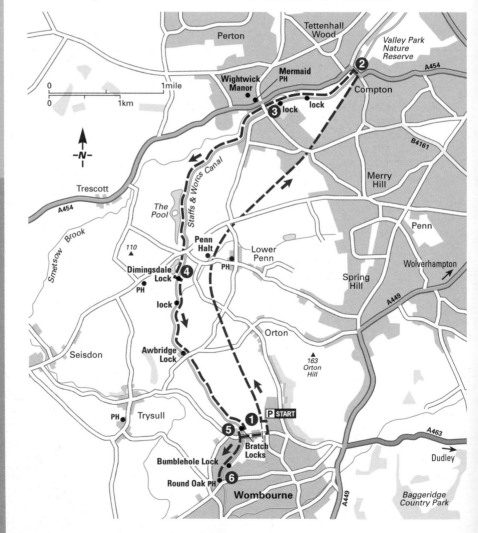

The Round Oak

about the pub

The Round Oak

100 Ounsdale Road, Wombourne
Wolverhampton, West Midlands
WV5 8BU
Tel: 01902 892083

DIRECTIONS: beside the canal at Ounsdale Bridge (see Point **5**)	
PARKING: 45	
OPEN: daily; all day	
FOOD: daily; all day Saturday & Sunday; all day School Holidays	
BREWERY/COMPANY: Banks Brewery	
REAL ALE: Banks Bitter & Original	

This big and busy family dining pub situated beside the Staffordshire and Worcester Canal was built to provide refreshment to the workers constructing the canal in the late 18th century. Extended in recent years it comprises several comfortably modernised dining areas, including a spacious bar area where locals congregate to sample pints of Marston's and Banks's beers. Expect a warm and friendly welcome, especially towards children.

Food

A standard pub food menu lists traditional bar snacks alongside a range of steaks, ples (cheese and potato, cottage pie), and a choice of fish dishes.

Family facilities

Very popular with families as it provides an indoor family room for dining, a children's menu and high chairs, while outside there's a play area and a bouncy castle.

Alternative refreshment stops

There's a café in the former station beside the car park at Wombourne, the Oddfellows at Compton, the Mermaid pub at Wightwick and a café if visiting Wightwick Manor.

☞ Where to go from here

Stop off at Wightwick Manor, one of the finest examples of 19th-century decorative style, where all aspects of William Morris's talents are shown in the house (www.nationaltrust.org.uk). Head for the Black Country Living Museum in Dudley, a re-created canalside village on a 26-acre (10.5ha) site. Meet the costumed guides and find out what life was like around 1900. Ride on a tramcar, take a trip down the underground mine, venture into the limestone caverns and visit the olde tyme fairground (www.bclm.co.uk).

Wombourne WEST MIDLANDS

Foxton Locks and the Grand Union Canal

Enjoy varied and challenging traffic-free riding along one of England's most famous canal systems.

Foxton Locks and the Grand Union Canal

The Grand Union Canal actually started its life as lots of separate canals, which were joined to provide a navigable waterway from Birmingham to London (the name 'Grand Union' comes from the amalgamation of a number of different companies in 1926). In 1793, long before this name was coined, a canal was begun in Leicester to link up with the Grand Junction Canal, which had started north from the Thames a year earlier. In 1814, the two were finally joined by the ten locks at Foxton, which raised the level of the Leicester canal by some 75ft (22.8m). It takes about 50 minutes for a boat to negotiate all ten locks, and each boat requires about 25,000 gallons of water. The history of the locks is explained in more detail at the Foxton Locks Museum (www.fipt.org.uk), near the start of the ride.

Also worth exploring is Millfield Wood, one of 200 woods created around the country as part of the Woods on Your Doorstep Project to celebrate the Millennium. The 18.8-acre (7.6ha) site was acquired by the Woodland Trust after a successful fund-raising appeal by Fleckney Village. Oak,

ash, silver birch and small numbers of field maple are the dominant species.

the ride

1 From the car park exit, turn left along a gravel track to get to the **bridge** over the canal. Cross the bridge and turn right to reach the **canal** and, after about 300m (330 yards), the **locks** themselves. Cycling isn't permitted on this section, so you'll have to walk your bikes down the side of the locks (the Foxton Locks Museum is situated on the far side of the passing pond about half-way down this long, steep slope, and can be reached on foot). Stay to the left at the bottom to reach the shop and **café**.

2 Continue past the shop to cross a **cobbled bridge**. On the far side, keep going in the same direction. The shingle track along this part of the canal is wide and smooth, although there are one or two places where the left hand edge has collapsed a little, so it's a good idea to stay right. After 1.5 miles (2km), you come to **Debdale Wharf**. Beyond Debdale Wharf, the path becomes narrow and grassy, and on dry days it may be quite bumpy. In the summer, this section may also be quite overgrown with reeds and bull-rushes, but it should still be passable. At **Gumley Road**, the track becomes smoother and wider again, before continuing on to **Saddington Road**.

3 Just beyond Saddington Road, a short sharp climb takes you up to the right

The towpath of the Grand Union Canal

2h00 — **9.6 MILES** — **15.5 KM** — **LEVEL 1 2 3**

MAP: OS Explorer 223 Northampton & Market Harborough

START/FINISH: Foxton Locks car park; grid ref: SP692892

TRAILS/TRACKS: smooth gravel, narrow grassy track, road and rutted farm track

LANDSCAPE: towpath, village and farmland

PUBLIC TOILETS: at the start

TOURIST INFORMATION: Market Harborough, tel 01858 821270

CYCLE HIRE: none locally

THE PUB: The Bell Inn, Gumley

🍴 A fairly challenging ride along an often bumpy towpath and some rough tracks – mountain bikes recommended. One short, steep descent to a railing over the canal (can easily be walked). Care is required crossing Kibworth Road. Suitable for older, more experienced and adventurous children

Getting to the start

Foxton is well signed off the A6 between Leicester and Market Harborough, off the A4304 to the west of Market Harborough, and off the B6047 to the north of Market Harborough. From Foxton, follow signs for the Foxton Locks car park, which is at the top end of the locks.

Why do this cycle ride?

This ride provides the perfect challenge to budding young mountain bikers, combining easy gravel towpath, flat grassy single tracks, a few gentle climbs, and some rough farm roads at the end of an alternative return route. The wonderfully preserved locks at the start are merely an added bonus.

Researched and written by: Paul Grogan

Foxton Locks LEICESTERSHIRE

of **Saddington Tunnel**. A longer but more gentle rise, still on a wide gravel track, then takes you along the top of the tunnel, before an equally gentle descent carries you back down to **Kibworth Road**. From here it's possible to return the way you came, but what follows is an alternative for those who are still feeling energetic.

4 If the gate is locked here, you'll have to carry your bikes over a **narrow stile**, before crossing the road with care to reach another, wider stile. Another gradual downhill then takes you to a short, steep slope down to a **fence** above the canal. This can be ridden, but you may prefer to walk it. At the fence turn left to continue along the canal. The path is quite narrow, and can be slippery in wet weather, so take great care here. At the next **bridge**, continue past it for about 30 yards to reach a gate – go through this gate to reach the bridge.

5 Cross the bridge and continue to the top of the field ahead, where you'll find an enormous slab of granite welcoming you to **Millfield Wood**. Go through a gate and continue along a wide bridleway across a field. Follow the track as it bears left to reach **Kibworth Road** and then cross the road to continue in the same direction along another **gravel track**.

6 After 1.5 miles (2km) of gentle downhill riding on a wide, occasionally pot-holed **track**, turn right at the road in **Smeeton**, and then first left along Debdale Lane. This rough **farm track** rises gently and then more steeply to reach the canal. At the top of the track, bear left towards **Debdale Wharf Farm** and then turn right at the farm to regain the **towpath**. From here, turn left to retrace your tracks back to the start.

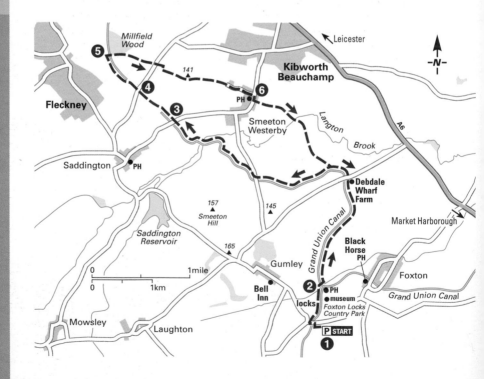

The Bell Inn

about the pub

The Bell Inn
2 Main Street, Gumley
Market Harborough, Leicestershire
LE16 7RU
Tel: 0116 279 2476

DIRECTIONS: signposted off the A6 north west of Market Harborough

PARKING: 20

OPEN: closed Sunday evening

FOOD: no food Monday evening

BREWERY/COMPANY: free house

REAL ALE: Greene King IPA, Timothy Taylor Landlord

Note the collection of miniature cricket bats in a case in the lobby as you enter this early 19th-century village pub. Beyond lies an L-shaped bar furnished with dark wood tables and chairs and decorated by more cricket bats and cricketing prints and cartoons, china jugs and mugs, hunting prints, and gleaming horse brasses on black beams. You'll also find a good range of beers, a warming log fire and a small no-smoking dining room. There is a pretty summer garden that is ideal for al fresco eating and drinking.

Food

Good value bar meals take in sandwiches, ploughman's lunches, home-made soups, salmon mornay, steaks and home-made puddings like sherry trifle. Popular three-course Sunday roast lunches.

Family facilities

Children over 10 are welcome in the restaurant but not in the terraced garden to the rear of the pub.

Alternative refreshment stops

Cold drinks, ice-creams and hot and cold snacks are available from the shop at Foxton Locks.

☞ Where to go from here

Market Harborough is a very picturesque medieval town with an interesting local museum and is well worth a visit if you have an hour or two to spare. Further afield, up the A6 to Leicester and a must if you have children in tow, is the National Space Centre

(www.nssc.co.uk), which offers five themed galleries, cutting-edge audio-visual technology and glimpses into genuine space research. More great cycling and walking can also be found on the Brampton Valley Way, which starts behind the Bell pub, on the A508 near the southern edge of Market Harborough.

Foxton Locks LEICESTERSHIRE

Through the Teme Valley

Seeking out the valleys amongst the Shropshire Hills.

Leintwardine

The lane out of Leintwardine takes you below a prominent hill on the right, on which there are the earthbank remains of a large Iron Age stronghold. When the Romans arrived in the area around 50 AD, they too recognised its importance and, in addition to taking it over, established another camp, Bravonium, by the river where the village now stands. In fact the church actually straddles one of the ramparts. The camp lay on a Roman road, Welsh Watling Street, between Wroxeter (near Shrewsbury) and Caerleon (outside

Newport), and was an important military route to help maintain order amongst the British tribes that still held strong in Wales. The road was also an imperial post road, and the camp was the equivalent of a stage post, supplying fresh horses and refreshment to speed the messengers on their way. During the calmer period of the 3rd century, the military presence declined, but by then, a civilian settlement had already sprung up, thriving on the trade that passed up and down the road.

Leintwardine's large church is known locally as the 'Cathedral of North Herefordshire'. It contains early 15th-century choir stalls with interestingly carved misericords, said to have come

Left: Time to check the map at a road junction

from the Augustinian Wigmore Abbey, which stood close to Paytoe Hall. In the churchyard of Burrington Church are a number of unusual cast-iron grave slabs, marking the burial sites of important local iron-founding families. During the 17th and early 18th centuries, iron was smelted using charcoal, and the surrounding forests were managed to provide abundant supplies of fuel.

the ride

1 Leaving **Petchfield Farm**, go right towards the hamlet of Elton, shortly passing a narrow lane off on the right called **Killhorse Lane**. You will soon discover the appropriateness of its name if you turn up it on your bike, for it has just about the steepest gradient in the area. Thankfully your route bends left, signed to Ludlow, soon taking you past a splendid manor house, **Elton Hall**.

2 At the next junction, turn off left, signed **'Burrington and Leintwardine'**, along a narrower lane, where occasional breaks in the hedges allow views across the valley to a backdrop of rolling hills. Before long the road begins to lose height, soon passing a lane off to the right, some 150yds (137m) along which you will find the entrance to **Burrington Church**. The route, however, continues ahead, the lane by now a leafy tunnel formed by a profuse growth of hazels on either side. Keep ahead past a turning to Leinthall Starkes to cross a bridge over the **Teme**, ignoring successive turnings to Downton a little later on and eventually reaching a junction by **Nacklestone Farm**.

MAP: OS Explorer 203 Ludlow, Tenbury Wells & Cleobury Mortimer

START/FINISH: Petchfield Farm, Elton; grid ref: SO454704 (small charge for parking)

TRAILS/TRACKS: quiet lanes throughout

LANDSCAPE: gentle valley amidst rolling hills

PUBLIC TOILETS: none on route

TOURIST INFORMATION: Ludlow, tel 01584 875053

CYCLE HIRE: Wheely Wonderful Cycling, Petchfield Farm, Elton, Ludlow, tel 01568 770755 (www.wheelywonderfulcycling.co.uk)

THE PUB: The Lion Hotel, Leintwardine

🚴 Narrow country lanes, be aware of traffic and pedestrians

Getting to the start

Petchfield Farm, some 5 miles (8km) south west of Ludlow, is most easily approached from the A4110 at Wigmore along a minor lane east through Leithnall Starkes. You will find the entrance to Petchfield Farm on the right after a mile (1.6km). Park in the yard beside 'Wheely Wonderful Cycle Hire'.

Why do this cycle ride?

The country lanes around Ludlow offer superb cycling, and although the general landscape is quite hilly, there are many easy routes that follow the base of the valleys. This one explores the valley of the River Teme between Elton and Leintwardine, and at one point follows the line of an important Roman road.

Researched and written by: Dennis Kelsall

The 14th-century clock tower of the Church of St Mary Magdalene at Leintwardine

3 Leintwardine is signed to the right, the way falling easily and soon affording a view to the village, the church with its sturdy tower an obvious feature. At a **T-junction**, sweep left with the main lane, and carry on to the end where there is a riverside green opposite **The Lion Hotel**.

4 Turn left over an arched bridge to re-cross the River Teme, and then go left again just beyond onto a narrow lane

signed to **Paytoe**. After passing a couple of **yards** on the outskirts of the village, the way continues in an almost dead-straight line along the flat valley floor following the line of a Roman road.

5 When you reach a junction, turn left in front of the splendid black-and-white **Paytoe Hall**, and pedal across the width of the valley, directed towards Ludlow. After crossing the Teme once more, go right and for a short while retrace your outward route. Just after the next bridge, turn off right to **Leinthall Starkes** and begin a short climb out of the valley that levels off to offer a view ahead to a **windmill** on the hillside above Leinthall. The lane bends sharp right and later left to drop towards the village.

6 When you reach a T-junction at the end go left, the lane undulating gently downwards along the valley side to take you back to **Petchfield Farm**.

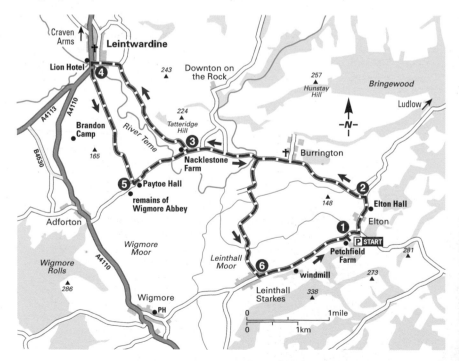

The Lion Hotel

The Lion enjoys an attractive riverside location by the bridge opposite the village green, and at the back has a peaceful, landscaped garden overlooking the River Teme and Brockley Meadow. It dates back to the 18th century when it was a thriving hotel and, although no longer residential, the building retains much of its character both in appearance and in the traditional hospitality offered by the hosts.

Food

Wide-ranging menus using local produce wherever possible take in lunchtime sandwiches, baguettes, standard bar snacks, various pies and grills, and specials like venison, home-made steak and kidney pie and vegetable curry. On Sundays, you'll find a choice of roasts, and there is a regular barbecue in summer.

Family facilities

Children of all ages are welcomed inside the Lion Hotel and there's a children's menu available.

about the pub

The Lion Hotel
High Street, Leintwardine, Ludlow
Shropshire SY7 0JZ
Tel: 01547 540203

DIRECTIONS: close to Leintwardine Bridge over the River Teme on the A4113 (see Point **3**)	
PARKING: 40	
OPEN: daily; all day Saturday	
FOOD: daily	
BREWERY/COMPANY: Enterprise Inns	
REAL ALE: changing guest beers	

Alternative refreshment stops

The Sun at Leintwardine (Rosemary Lane) is an unspoiled gem and worth a visit for Woods tapped from the barrel, but no food is available there.

☞ Where to go from here

Spend some time exploring the extensive range of ruined buildings at Ludlow Castle (www.ludlowcastle.com), where audio guides bring the castle to life. Discover the secrets of the Shropshire Hills at the Discovery Centre in Craven Arms, where the history, nature and geography of the area is explored through a series of interactive displays and simulations, all housed in a striking building set in 25 acres (10ha) of meadows (www.shropshireonline.gov.uk/discover.nsf). Visit Stokesay Castle, a perfectly preserved 13th-century fortified manor house – stroll through the great hall and delightful cottage gardens.

Baddesley Clinton and Packwood House

Ride along towpaths that connect two old houses.

Ancient houses

The Stratford-upon-Avon Canal created a route between the Worcester Canal at Kings Norton Junction, just south of Birmingham, and the River Avon at Stratford. Authorised by an Act of Parliament in 1793, the upper section to Hockley Heath was soon completed, but a shortage of funds delayed construction of the costly locks taking the canal downhill into the Avon valley. The waterway only reached Kingswood in 1802 and was not finally completed until 1816. A cut at Kingswood joined the Stratford to the Warwick and Birmingham Canal, which lay just to the east and was absorbed within the Grand Union system during the 1920s. Although commercial traffic continued on the Grand Union into the 1960s, the closure of the Avon Navigation in 1873 dealt a harsh blow to the Stratford Canal's fortunes and by the 1930s the section below Lapworth was derelict.

Centred like a jewel within its 13th-century moat, Baddesley Clinton has one of the most picturesque settings in the country. Slender Tudor chimneys of ornate brick rise above the roof, while below, the stonework of the inner sanctum gives way to half-timbering overlooking a delightful courtyard garden secluded from the world. Inside is no less a delight; elaborately carved chimney pieces and wood-panelled walls decorate rooms that are elegantly furnished to represent different periods in the life of the house, whilst shimmering reflections dance off the water through mullioned windows onto the ceilings.

Formerly held by the Benedictine priory of Coventry, Packwood passed into secular ownership following Henry VIII's Dissolution of the monasteries in the 1530s. The splendid many-gabled and chimneyed manor house was erected by the Fetherstones towards the end of the 16th century, originally a timber-frame building, but subsequently 'modernised' with a rendered brick façade. Inside, however, it is infused with the charm of its early period. Its last owner, Graham Ash, carefully restored the building and scoured the neighbourhood rescuing authentic furnishings and fittings from the break up or demolition of other ancient houses. He, too, is partly responsible for the yew garden, for which the house is famous, extending the mid-17th-century topiary towards the house in an arrangement that has since become known as 'The Sermon on the Mount'.

2h00 **9.75 MILES** **15.7 KM** **LEVEL 123**

the ride

1 Join the Stratford-upon-Avon Canal behind the car park, turn right past a lock to a **bridge** where the canal splits. Cross to the spur, which drops through a second lock to another bridge, there dismounting to descend **four steps** on the far side. Follow the **towpath** away from the junction, passing a picnic site and going beneath a railway bridge to meet the **Grand Union Canal**.

2 Cycle along the towpath to the right for some 0.75 mile (1.2km) to the second **bridge (No. 63)**, leaving immediately beyond it for the lane above. Over the bridge, climb away past the Tom O' The Wood pub. At a **'Give Way'** crossroads, keep ahead over the **B4439**, enjoying easy pedalling for a little over 0.5 mile (800m) to the end of the lane.

3 To the left, the way leads past **Hay Wood**, eventually meeting another junction. Go left again towards Lapworth and **Baddesley Clinton**, the lane shortly falling to pass the entrance of Baddesley Clinton, which lies opposite Netherwood Lane. Turn in beside the **lodge** and follow the winding drive to a car park at its end. The National Trust has provided separate facilities for cycles, enabling you to explore the house and nearby church on foot.

4 Returning to the main lane, turn left towards **Hockley Heath**, soon dropping to a blind humpback bridge spanning the

MAP: OS Explorer 220 Birmingham & Explorer 221 Coventry & Warwick

START/FINISH: Kingswood; car park in Brome Hall lane; grid ref: SP185710

TRAILS/TRACKS: quiet lanes and canal towpaths with predominantly gravel surfaces

LANDSCAPE: hedged lanes and canals winding through rolling agricultural countryside

PUBLIC TOILETS: at the start

TOURIST INFORMATION: Solihull, tel 0121 704 6130

CYCLE HIRE: Clarkes Cycle Shop, Henley Street and Guild Street, Stratford-upon-Avon, tel 01789 205057, www.cycling-tours.org.uk

THE PUB: The Boot Inn, Lapworth

🛈 Traffic on country lanes, one awkward right-hand turn, low bridges and overhanging branches along towpath

Getting to the start

From M42, junction 4, follow the A3400 south in the direction of Stratford. Passing through Hockley Heath, bear left onto the B4439, continuing for 2.5 miles (4km) to Kingswood. Shortly after passing The Boot Inn turn right into Brome Hall lane. The car park entrance is on the left.

Why do this cycle ride?

At Kingswood, two separate canals came within yards of each other. Their towpaths provide an off-road link in this enjoyable ride that visits two nearby ancient houses.

Researched and written by: Dennis Kelsall

Top right: The Stratford-upon-Avon Canal
Left: Packwood House

Baddesley Clinton

WARWICKSHIRE

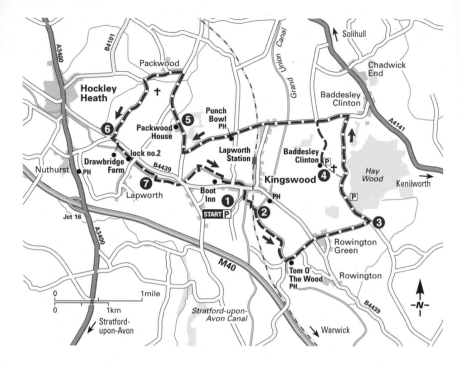

Grand Union Canal. Beyond there, keep going over a railway bridge and later, ahead at a crossroads beside the **Punch Bowl**. About 0.5 mile (800m) further on, the road turns sharply left. Exercising caution, turn off right onto a narrow lane leading past **Packwood House**, which stands beside the road only a short distance along.

5 Resuming your ride, carry on for almost another 0.75 mile (1.2km) to the second lane leaving on the left, **Vicarage Road**. It is signed to Packwood and Hockley Heath. Follow that for 0.5 mile (800m) and then turn left at an unsigned junction. Winding past Packwood's church, **St Giles**, the lane eventually ends at a main road, the B4439.

6 Turn left towards **Lapworth and Warwick**, but after 200 yards (182m) and just before some **white cottages**, swing off right onto a gravel track, the entrance to **Drawbridge Farm**. Meeting the canal a few

yards/metres along, follow the towpath left to the first of a long series of **locks** (No. 2) heralding the canal's descent to **Kingswood**. Prudent cyclists will then dismount to negotiate the sharp dip and low ridge immediately beyond the lock.

7 The path crosses to the opposite bank over a bridge below **lock No. 4**, remaining on that side to pass beneath a road bridge and shortly reaching **lock No. 6**. Beyond, locks then follow in quick succession, forming a staircase that drops the canal some 70ft (21m) in little over 0.5 mile (800m). The towpath reverts to the north bank below **lock No. 7**, recrossing once more after lock No. 14, where **The Boot Inn** lies, just along a track south of the canal. The final stretch continues along the towpath beneath a road bridge, bending past four more locks and under a final **bridge** to return you to the ride's starting point at the car park.

The Boot Inn

Barely a stone's throw from the Grand Union Canal, the 16th-century Boot is a rustic and rambling brick building that became a pub when the canal was built some 200 years ago. Much of its early trade came from the canal, busy with cargo to Birmingham. Today it is a lively and convivial place, the smart refurbished bar with timbered ceilings, quarry-tiled floors and glowing fires, drawing diners from far and wide for modern brasserie-style food and interesting global wines. There's an attractive summer garden with a canopy and patio heaters for those cooler evenings. The inn sign depicts a caricature by renowned artist, Jim Bulmer, known for his humorous cartoons of local characters.

about the pub

The Boot Inn
Old Warwick Road, Lapworth,
Warwickshire B94 6JU
Tel: 01564 782464
www.thebootatlapworth.co.uk

DIRECTIONS: See Getting to the start and point **7** of the ride

PARKING: 60

OPEN: daily; all day

FOOD: daily

BREWERY/COMPANY: Enterprise Inns

REAL ALE: Bass, Wadworth 6X, Greene King Old Speckled Hen

Food

Food is freshly prepared and the new a la carte menu served lunchtime and evening takes in 'first plates' like rustic breads with roast garlic and olive oil or bubble and squeak with poached egg and bacon with Hollandaise, with main dishes ranging from seared fillet of seabass with crab and lemon aioli. Sandwiches and specials are served at lunchtime.

Family facilities

Children are most welcome inside the pub. There's a children's menu and both smaller portions of adult dishes and high chairs are available.

Alternative refreshment stops

The Punch Bowl and Tom O' The Wood pubs are along the route and there's a restaurant and tea room at Baddesley Clinton.

☞ Where to go from here

In addition to Packwood House and Baddesley Clinton (www.nationaltrust. org.uk), the area has two grand castles, Kenilworth and Warwick. The latter dominates the town and attractions include the gloomy dungeon and Torture Chamber, the grand State Rooms and Great Hall (www.warwick-castle.com). Shakespeare enthusiasts should head south to Stratford-upon-Avon and the surrounding villages – Mary Arden's house in Wilmcote and Anne Hathaway's Cottage in Shottery (www.shakespeare.org.uk).

Baddesley Clinton

WARWICKSHIRE

Around Pitsford Water

Look out for the abundant birdlife along this purpose-built, waterfront cycle track.

The Reservoir

Established in 1997 with the help of a substantial grant from the Millennium Fund, Brixworth is the newest country park in Northamptonshire, while Pitsford Water was designated as a Site of Special Scientific Interest (or SSSI) in 1971. The latter is home to numerous species of wading birds, is the site of the county's largest winter gull roost, and is regularly visited by ospreys on their spring migrations. In the winter, wildfowl numbers have been known to reach 10,000, with ducks, grebes, geese and swans being the most common residents. The wide variety of habitats around the reservoir also provides food and shelter for migrant birds in spring – surveys show a breeding population of 55 species.

In the summer, meanwhile, the reserve comes alive with dragonflies and damselflies. Common blue and emerald damselflies are probably the most abundant species, with each numbering many hundreds of

thousands on a good day. Butterflies add to the colour with 23 different species recorded. Other attractions at the park include a brand new playground, a sensory garden, a boules area (balls are available for hire), three wheel-chair accessible nature trails and a human sundial. Sailing, windsurfing and canoeing lessons are available from the Marina (April to October) and fly fishing can be arranged at the Lodge on Holcot Causeway (the reservoir is stocked with 35,000 trout each year).

the ride

1 From the main exit of the car park, turn left on a **gravel track**, following the obvious cycle path signs. Take this track down towards the water's edge, heading to the right of the **playground**, until you reach the **main cycle track** around the reservoir, with the marina off to your right.

2 Turn left here, along the wide and smooth gravel track, following the water's edge. You shortly pass through a sequence of gates and continue to follow the shore around a

Watersports on Pitsford Water

1h30 — **7.5 MILES** — **12 KM** — **LEVEL 123**

MAP: OS Explorer 223 Northampton & Market Harborough

START/FINISH: Brixworth Country Park car park; grid ref: SP752695

TRAILS/TRACKS: smooth gravel or tarmac all the way round

LANDSCAPE: woodland, waterside and causeway

PUBLIC TOILETS: at the start

TOURIST INFORMATION: Northampton, tel 01604 622677

CYCLE HIRE: Pitsford Water Cycle Hire, tel 01604 881777

THE PUB: The White Horse, Old Northampton

⚠ Care needs to be taken when exiting the car park at the west end of the causeway

Getting to the start

Brixworth Country park is signed from the A508 between Market Harborough and Northampton. The route starts at the visitor centre on the reservoir's western shore just to the south of Brixworth.

Why do this cycle ride?

This is a gentle and enjoyable ride on smooth gravel tracks. With great views of the reservoir and little in the way of hills or other challenges to contend with, it's ideal for families with younger children.

Researched and written by: Paul Grogan

series of **shallow bays**. As the reservoir starts to narrow, you come to the first gradual rise of the ride, followed by the option of a quick up-and-down single track for the more adventurous. This whole stretch is dotted with little coves, benches and **picnic tables**, while signs along the water's edge warn of the necessity to watch out for back-casting by anglers.

3 Within sight of the causeway, proceed through another **swing gate**, and then just before you reach the causeway, go through another gate and over a **cattle grid** to reach a car park and picnic area (during the summer, there may be an ice-cream van here, providing the perfect excuse for a rest). This is also a good place for a spot of bird watching.

4 Take care when exiting the car park to reach the cycle path across the **causeway** (this path, which is marked with a bike symbol, is on the car park side of the causeway, so you don't need to cross the main road). Continue to the end of the causeway and up a short rise.

An orientation sign at Pitsford Water

5 Just before the top of this gradual rise, turn right, through a gate and into some **woods**. Enjoy the ride's first little stretch of downhill through the trees, before negotiating a sweeping left-hand turn. Proceed through a gate and follow the water's edge into a long, narrow **inlet**. Go through a gate just before the end of the inlet. A tight turn at the end of the inlet will take you back along the other side.

6 Continue to skirt around the reservoir until you come to a corridor through some **trees**. Go through a gate and follow the track along the left-hand edge of a

wood until you reach a pair of gates and a tarmac road (to the left is **Moulton Grange**). Turn right on the road, over a miniature causeway. Immediately after the causeway, turn right again, back onto the **cycle track** (this is not well signed) and follow it around to the **dam**. Continue across the dam, taking a moment to soak in the expansive views of the reservoir. At the end of the dam, go through a gate and then turn right onto the wooded cycle track just past the **sailing club entrance**. At the end of the woods, you reach the point where you first joined the **main trail**. Turn left here to get back to the car park and the start.

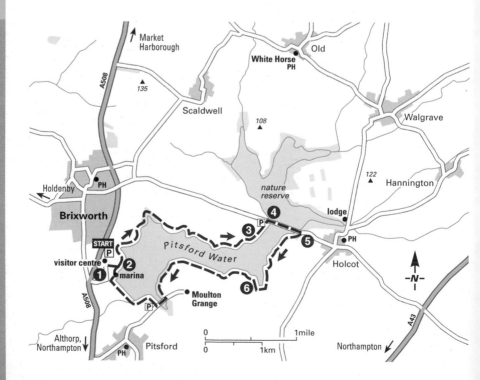

Pitsford Water

NORTHAMPTONSHIRE

The White Horse

Small, friendly village local in a superb village setting overlooking the 13th-century St Andrew's church, a view best appreciated from the lovely enclosed garden which also features a fine restored red-brick chimney. Inside, the character bar and comfortable lounge areas, are spotlessly maintained, with hunting prints and collections of china decorating the walls, and splendid log fires to cosy-up to on cold winter days.

Food

Traditional home-cooked meals range from good-value sandwiches and filled baguettes to lamb and mint suet pudding, spinach and ricotta cannelloni, grilled tuna steak, and beef Wellington. Regular theme nights.

Family facilities

Children are welcome in the bars.

Alternative refreshment stops

A wide selection of hot and cold snacks and meals are available from the Willow Tree Café at the start. Ice creams may be available at the causeway car park during the summer, and snacks and hot and cold refreshments are available from the nature reserve lodge, near the eastern end of the causeway.

☛ Where to go from here

Holdenby House, about 4 miles (6.4km) to the west of the reservoir, boasts a splendid Elizabethan garden and a falconry centre (www.holdenby.com). Also nearby, about the same distance to the south, is the Northampton and Lampton Railway, on the Brampton Valley Way, just to the east of Chapel Brampton (www.nlr.org.uk). About five miles (8km) to the southwest is Althorp, the final resting place of Diana Princess of Wales (www.althorp.com).

about the pub

The White Horse

Walgrave Road, Old
Northampton, Northamptonshire
NN6 9QX
Tel: 01604 781297

DIRECTIONS: Old is located north of Northampton between the A508 and A43; pub is in the village centre next to the church

PARKING: 10

OPEN: closed Monday & Tuesday lunchtime

FOOD: daily

BREWERY/COMPANY: Banks Brewery

REAL ALE: Banks's Bitter, two guest beers

Pitsford Water

NORTHAMPTONSHIRE

Stratford Greenway

Explore the quiet countryside in which the world's greatest bard grew up.

Stratford-upon-Avon

Whilst Stratford was already a prosperous town before William Shakespeare's day, it is probably due to his association and his worldwide reputation that so many of the town's splendid 16th-century buildings have survived. Some of the best line Church Street, along which the ride finishes. Buildings include a splendid row of almshouses, the early 15th-century Guild Hall and Grammar School (where Shakespeare is said to have been educated), some impressive inns and the site of New Place, where the poet died in 1616. Stop off too to look in Holy Trinity Church, where he was both baptised and buried.

The ride out follows the route of the Oxford, Worcester and Wolverhampton Railway, built in 1859 to link the Midlands with the south west of England. A decade and a half later, another line was constructed to the town from the south east, with junctions and sidings in the area now occupied by Swan Meadow car park and a separate station to service the racecourse. As the country's rail network developed, the smaller lines were absorbed, the Great Western buying up the Midlands line whilst the London, Midland and Scottish Railway took over the other. Bringing tourists to the town from the capital, the latter became known as the 'Shakespeare Route', but closed in 1965 as part of Beeching's rationalisation programme. The GWR, along which the Greenway now runs, was taken up in 1976, leaving only the route from the north into the town.

the ride

1 Leave Clopton Bridge along Waterside, passing the **Royal Shakespeare Theatre** and famous Dirty Duck pub. Turn left at the end to wind past Holy Trinity Church and then go left again into **Mill Lane**. It finishes in a narrow alley, usually busy with pedestrians, that leads to the river. The continuing path swings beneath a **bridge** to shadow the main road, shortly passing **Seven Meadows car park**.

2 If joining the **railway track** at Seven Meadows, turn right to **Milcote picnic area**. The way runs beside Stratford's **racecourse** where, on race days, horses gallop along the back straight. The track then crosses the Avon by a riverside picnic area and later, the River Stour. Pedal on beyond **Chambers Halt** and Pearces Crossing to the pine-grown platform of **Milcote Station**.

3 Through barriers and a parking area, cross a road to a **picnic site** where an old railway coach houses a café. The track continues for a further 2 miles (3.2km), passing crossings at **Knobbs Farm** and the **Airfield** before ultimately reaching **Wyre Lane Crossing**. Leave there, going right along Wyre Lane into **Long Marston**. The

Safe family cycling on Stratford Railway Path

| 3h30 | 15.5 MILES | 25 KM | LEVEL 123 |

MAP: OS Explorer 205 Stratford-upon-Avon & Evesham

START/FINISH: Stratford: Clopton Bridge, grid ref SP203549 or Seven Meadows car park, grid ref SP195540

TRAILS/TRACKS: streets in Stratford and disused railway line with good gravel surface, country lanes and farm track

LANDSCAPE: patchwork fields of the Avon valley rising to a backdrop of low hills

PUBLIC TOILETS: in Stratford

TOURIST INFORMATION: Stratford, tel 0870 160 7930

CYCLE HIRE: Clarkes Cycle Shop, Henley Street and Guild Street, Stratford-upon-Avon; tel: 01789 205057; www.cycling-tours.org.uk

THE PUB: Masons Arms, Long Marston

⚠ Traffic on Stratford's busy streets and country lanes, pedestrians along the track

Getting to the start

Stratford-upon-Avon is close to junction 15 on the M40. If parking in the town, start the ride at Clopton Bridge, which brings the A422 into Stratford. Alternatively, begin from Seven Meadows car park on the A4390.

Why do this cycle ride?

Leaving Stratford-upon-Avon along the level track of a former railway line, the route leads to Long Marston, where the pub makes an excellent stop for lunch. Either return on the outward track or follow country lanes via the picturesque village of Welford-on-Avon.

Researched and written by: Dennis Kelsall

Mason's Arms is just a short way along the main road to the right.

4 To return, either retrace your outward route, or alternatively, instead of going back along Wyre Lane, keep ahead on the road to the outskirts of the village. There, turn off right to **Dorsington**, passing the church of **St James the Great**. Carry on for 1.5 miles (2.4km) to a T-junction and go right, winding to another junction in the middle of Dorsington. Take the lane on the right to **Welford**, which snakes north between the fields, culminating in a short, stiff pull to give a view across the Avon valley. Drop to a road and follow that right into modern Welford. However, leave after just over 0.5 mile (800m) along **Headland Road** on the left, which ends in the old village opposite **St Peter's Church**.

5 The onward route lies to the right along **Church Street**, but first wander down Boat Lane to see its thatched black and white cottages. At the end of Church Street by the **Bell Inn**, take the main road right through the village, passing a small green where there stands a tall **maypole**. Leaving Welford, turn off left to **Weston and Clifford Chambers**, going left again after 0.5 mile (800m) on a narrow lane to **Weston-on-Avon**.

Stratford-upon-Avon

WARWICKSHIRE

Stratford-upon-Avon WARWICKSHIRE

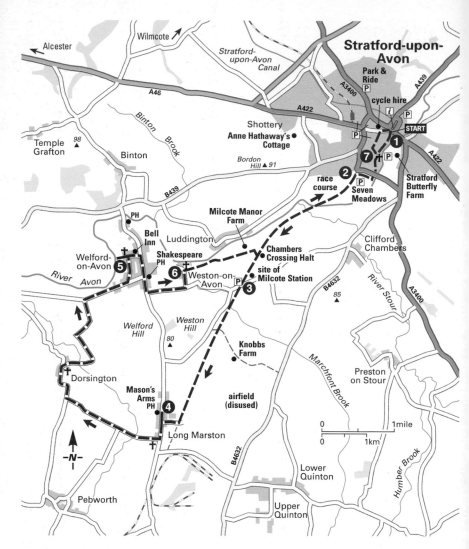

6 At the bottom turn right past the village **church**, the way deteriorating to a farm track as it continues between the fields beyond. Keep forward as it reverts to tarmac, later passing **Milcote Manor Farm** to a couple of **cottages**. The way disintegrates to dirt as it then swings right to meet the disused railway at **Chambers Crossing Halt**. Follow it left back to Seven Meadows car park and Stratford.

7 If you began from the town, after passing **Holy Trinity Church** you must now carry on past **Riverside** and instead turn right at the next crossroads into **Church Street**. Continue ahead along Chapel Street and **High Street** to a busy roundabout in the town centre, where you might wish to dismount to return to your car park.